Bag Girl:
Home is Where the Bag Is

by: Tozaneé Shanteesé Smith

Copyright ©2023 Tozaneé Shanteesé Smith

All rights reserved.

ISBN 9798218197841

To be printed in the United States. This publication is not designed to provide accurate and authoritative information regarding the subject matter covered. It is sold with the understanding that the author/publisher is not engaged in rendering any professional service or advice. If professional care is required, then the expert assistance of a competent, qualified authoritarian should be sought.

This book, or parts thereof, may not be reproduced in any form, stored in any retrieval system, or transmitted in any form by any means—electronic, mechanical, photocopy, recording, or otherwise—without prior written permission of the author, except as provided by United States of America copyright law.

Smith, Tozaneé Shanteesé

Bag Girl: Home is Where the Bag Is / Smith, Tozaneé Shanteesé / Non-Fiction / Memoir

Dedication

I dedicate this book to all the people who never thought I would amount to anything. Thank you for giving me the strength I needed to keep moving forward each and every day.

Table of Contents

Prologue 7

Chapter 1: Bag Girl 17

Chapter 2: The Black Kid 20

Chapter 3: Ernesto 24

Chapter 4: The Wedding 27

Chapter 5: Coming of Age 31

Chapter 6: High School, Sex, and Drugs 35

Chapter 7: A Father's Love 43

Chapter 8: The Game Plan 47

Chapter 9: Senior Year 73

Chapter 10: F.A.T. 100

Chapter 11: Graduation 115

Chapter 12: Not So Virgin Mary .132

Chapter 13: The Beginning of an End 147

About the Author 165

Acknowledgments .... .166

Prologue
Christmas Eve 2020

There's safety in familiarity, even if what's familiar isn't what you'd consider ideal. It was what I reminded myself of as I pulled into the Motel 6 parking lot and looked up at the neon sign that cast a faint, sickly glow on the faded asphalt below. The brick was also faded, and this structure that housed the broken, the broke, and the just plain dejected was looking like a forgotten slice of the town everyone simply drove by.

But to me, this was it.

This was the familiar. It often came to feel like home if only for the simple fact that I had found peace here many times over the last few years in my twenties, falling short of what popular sitcoms and songs had promised me, in a small, snug room that had no space for toxicity to creep in and catch me unguarded. I had to pay either nightly or weekly to be the master of my own domain, however small that domain might be. It was more than many others could claim for themselves, from the homeless out on the street to those crowded in shelters. I was lucky to be in neither category, though at this moment, luck felt like it was in short supply.

On this night, as Christmas Eve slowly faded into Christmas Day, this safe haven beckoned me to come in after I'd fucked up badly earlier in the day with my Nana. I had a place with her, and now I didn't. Like a dam split open, my anger and my PTSD from a life lived as if walking on broken glass filled the apartment until we were both yelling at each other, and I had no option but to pack my stuff and leave, slamming the door on her obscenities and disappointments. The memory of how the day had started sat behind my eyes, stinging. I shook my head as if to toss the images aside but to no avail. Instead, I felt a dull headache coming on, and the shaking only exacerbated the throbbing.

Flurries began to fall, and for a moment, I reveled at the sight of it, at the perfect timing of it to come down on Christmas Eve. But then, as if someone flipped a switch, I suddenly thought, *Who gives a shit?* Around me, my car was packed with my belongings, and I sat among them, tucked in behind the wheel like another object in the heap.

Living at my Nana's place felt less like a privilege and a comfort and more like an inconvenience to her, but even as we coexisted like two meteors barely missing each other in the small space, there were clashes. As she was the mother of my own absent mother, I had come to expect much of the same from her. Though, to give her credit, she was at least present, even if her presence was marred with biting sarcasm and sharply pointed words meant to cut open.

Still.

She let me stay with her when I had no other home, and for that exceedingly small, very meager act of kindness, I maintained some level of gratitude, even if that gratitude was misplaced. Nana never let me forget that everything about my existence was temporary.

I did not have my own bedroom. No closet either. Well, the closet I did have, but the way I used it reminded me that this was only a temporary situation, and I was my grandmother's guest. Hidden in the closet sat my large trash bag, filled with toiletries and clothes that I'd dig around in each morning before heading to the bathroom with an armful of items that threatened to spill onto the tile floor... Each morning, I'd get up from the couch and put away all evidence that a sleeping body had kept it warm all night. In my gratitude lived the realization that my Nana's invitation was only as good as my mild mannerisms and tidiness. Out of sight, out of mind.

On the morning that brought me to Motel 6, I woke up too early, long before my alarm was expected to go off, and once I was awake, there was no going back to sleep. It was initially the sound of *The Andy Griffith Show* theme song that jolted me awake. It was the only DVD set Nana owned and, like comfort food on a sick day, she'd turn to it each night before bed, often falling asleep with the sound still blaring. Hearing the theme song and knowing she found comfort in it was the only time I'd feel any real sense of warmth towards her.

While the sound had surprisingly become a comfort to me, its crackling through an otherwise quiet night annoyed me this time, though I didn't dare get up to turn it off. Instead, I turned towards the window and stared out at what I hoped would be an uneventful Christmas Eve.

I still had a few hours before my alarm would go off for work, and the more I willed myself to go back to sleep, the less tired I became. Instead, my mind whirred with memories of my childhood, of previous Christmases that I had also hoped would be joyful or surprising or, at the very least, boring. Instead, I recalled being a teenager and my mom informing me that I was too old to receive Christmas presents anymore, not unlike being told at my thirteenth birthday that it would be the last birthday we'd celebrate now that I was an adult.

I closed my eyes and hoped sleep would come, but instead, I found old disappointments and hurt bubbling to the surface.

The car had been running so long in the parking lot that the air coming from the vents was no longer warm and comforting. I had the radio on while driving there to keep my thoughts at bay, and I'd now noticed that I never turned it off. I'd only lowered the volume until it hit that low buzz like a fly trapped in a room. Whatever came on next had bells jingling in the background, and I wasn't in the mood for festive sounds, so I slapped my hand against the dial and turned off the radio.

Even in a place where I'm all too familiar, my instinct was to take in the scene: look around, inspect, and feel at ease before unlocking the door and stepping out. Old habits die hard, and much of how I operated was carried over from my childhood trauma. The need to check my surroundings never truly went away, even in adulthood.

Before turning off the car, I noticed a couple who was smoking and in deep conversation outside their motel room. It was too cold to be standing outside to smoke, but then I thought about how we find reprieve in the mundane and the familiar, even if it takes you outside on a winter's night, even if the act that brings you reprieve is an unhealthy one that fits in nicely with your anxiety. I didn't smoke, but I suddenly wished I could join them and ask them why they were here on a holiday. I wondered if we had more in common than not.

My eyes moved from the tired-looking couple to scan the unassuming building again. I saw a window on the top floor full of Christmas clings: snowmen and Santa with reindeer chasing after each other but only within the confines of the panes. I wondered how long that family had been living there to feel the need to decorate their windows, and as I began imagining who they were and what they were like—how many kids' spirits they needed to keep up—I felt a lump in the back of my throat as my own fear of not knowing how long I'd be here caught up with me. I was suddenly crying, and I wasn't sure whom I felt the saddest for—those kids or myself.

Even in the sadness of thinking about children spending their Christmas in a motel room, I found a quiet joy in that window scene that nearly broke me. *How nice,* I thought, *to have a family who wants to keep the joy of Christmas alive no matter the circumstances.* It was a thought that sent me spiraling down my own rabbit hole of the complicated mess that came with childhood abandonment and assault. My anger from earlier in the day flushed again, and while all I wanted to do was scream, I instead sobbed uncontrollably.

While most arguments started out small, mine felt like they went from zero to sixty in a matter of minutes. It began with tiptoeing around the dark apartment to make my way to the bathroom, careful not to wake my Nana while I got ready for work. My concentration on my morning routine and the hope that I left before she woke up was enough to keep me distracted from the bubbling anger over how I existed in this space.

I didn't flush the toilet until just before I was about to leave. I turned the faucet off while brushing and not rinsing. I breathed slowly, slowly, slowly, careful not to let out a sigh, so different from the exasperations and private outbursts I'd had as a kid. But you grow and you learn there are conditions all around you if you want to survive.

All my tiptoeing was for naught because before long, Nana was up. She was slamming pots and pans around the kitchen, grumbling under her breath, angry that I was ignoring her and that I was sneaking around the apartment to stay out of her hair. Her bad eyesight made her turn on every light in the apartment, and I felt strangely exposed standing in a space that had become my personal limbo.

"Toza! How come you're walkin' around here not speaking to me?" she yelled from the kitchen.

I stood in the living room by my couch, the one that now showed no sign of doubling as a bed, with my shoes on, ready to go to work, ready to put yet another holiday behind me.

"I took you in when you had nowhere else to go, and I'm the only one in this family who is willing to help you," she continued.

I wondered what kind of payment she expected from me for this one act of duty rather than kindness. She hit this angle from time-to-time, as if reminding herself more than me why I was allowed to live there and how lucky I was to be in her presence.

Though there were stark differences between my own mother and Nana, I could sometimes feel the two converge when Nana got loud, panicky, or downright mean, and the memories would come flooding back—memories of my mom sleeping off the previous night's party. Memories of learning how to feed my younger siblings when our mom disappeared for days on end, only to come back with a new boyfriend. Memories of feeling like an outsider in my own neighborhood and my own home.

At twenty-eight-years-old, I felt myself freefalling back to my childhood. Before I knew it, I was screaming back at Nana between tears about how I wasn't treated as human, as an equal in her own home—screaming until she shouted back in defiance, and we were both letting our lives' disparities and challenges fill the space until I felt like I was suffocating.

Nana was going on about how she didn't understand what I meant, about how I made it a point to keep her daughter away from her, and I was grabbing my few belongings from the closet before stepping outside for the last time and slamming the door behind me.

All my life, I'd tiptoed through spaces, eager to keep a peace that never existed. If there was no peace to find among people, I'd simply venture out to find it on my own, no matter the cost.

Inside the lobby, the fluorescent lights gave a yellow sheen to the room. As I imagined worst-case scenarios for myself—no rooms available, no one working the desk at this time on Christmas Eve—a beautiful Indigenous woman came out from the back office. I recognized her. She was always the one there when I'd checked myself in before. She saw me and smiled, and I fought the urge to smile back and make small talk as if we were old friends.

She probably smiles at everyone, I thought. *Why would I stand out from any other customer?*

"Can I help you?" she asked.

I looked at her with confusion on my face because I didn't know how anyone could help me. But I regained my composure, managed my sad-girl thoughts, and shakily said, "I need a room."

"Okay, how many people?"

"Just me."

Suddenly, I stumbled when she asked for how long. I felt my palms grow sweaty and the ball in the back of my throat grow. The moment felt like a long, endless stretch of empty road before I finally told her that I wasn't sure. She looked at me as if expecting something more, and I grew irrationally angry at this woman who didn't know anything about my life.

"I think a week," I finally managed in an attempt to take ownership of my situation again.

As the encounter came towards its end, I noticed how utterly exhausted I felt—mentally, physically, emotionally. I passed my credit card to the woman as I silently cursed myself for handing over the majority of my paycheck. I thought about how doomed I felt when I tried to look at my life objectively. I was age twenty-eight, damn near close to thirty, and things just continued to go downhill for me.

Stepping from flurries to a yellowed lobby to flurries again made this night feel more like a strange dream sequence, and as I walked to my room, I wondered how we could tell the difference between real life and a dream world. I thought about how maybe this was all just a bad dream. Perhaps, my whole life had been.

Once in my room, I methodically set things down and took a look around. It was just as I remembered it. The only constant in my life was the aesthetics of the Motel 6 room, and in some hilariously ridiculous way, I felt a little grateful for it.

At least the room is mine, I thought. *No sharing, no hiding my belongings in a quiet corner.* It was temporary, sure, but I was keen on finding reprieve in the quiet moments between the chaos.

After inspecting the bathroom and testing the TV to make sure it worked, I headed back into the cold to collect the rest of my belongings from my car. Not quite sure how long I'd be there, I decided to bring everything I had inside and make the most of this moment in my life. Focused on the task at hand, the brisk walk between car and room, car and room, I stayed preoccupied as I counted my steps, counted my breaths, and quickly walked past windows, most of which had the curtains drawn against the outside world. On my last trip back to my room, last trash bag in hand, I noticed one window that hadn't been covered. An older man sat inside with the light on, the neon blue of the TV reflecting against the glass. On a table near the window, I saw a lava lamp glowing against an otherwise drab room, and I couldn't help but smile.

Back in my room, showered and finally in bed with Christmas less than an hour away, I was too tired to continue mentally harping on my day's Sisyphean struggles. I had the TV on in the background playing some Hallmark holiday movie, and it was enough to keep me distracted as I felt myself slipping from wakefulness and hovering in the in-between. My mind began to tease me with half-memories of when my life felt like it was finally trending in the right direction and again with the moments that always threatened whatever security I was after.

This balancing act tested my strength, and all I could do before completely succumbing to sleep was remember that I was safe for the night, and I was here of my own free will. I checked my phone before turning back to the TV to find that it was just after midnight. It was Christmas, and outside, the snow was coming down harder. I thought about the kids in the room with the holiday clings and the man with his lava lamp. It was a hodgepodge quilt of families, sitting in limbo, and now, here I was thrown into the mix once again.

"Merry Christmas, Tozaneé," I whispered to myself before putting the phone back on the nightstand. I pulled the covers over my head and decided not to think past this moment. I sunk down further and forced myself to sleep, praying tomorrow wouldn't be another day that filled me with utter dread and regret.

Chapter 1
Bag Girl

Bag Girl, that's what she is; that's what they call her, and that's all she has. Bags have been her identity for the past five years. So, this is her story—my story, my confessions, my reveal. My name is Tozaneé Shanteesé Smith, and I am Bag Girl.

No one ever grows up thinking or knowing they will end up homeless, sleeping in their car, or trying to commit suicide. No one pictures their life that way. They envision beautiful, good times with friends and family, not their family turning their backs and leaving them to fend for themselves. But it happens, only to the worst of us.

My identity came about in the fall of 2015. It was September 2015 to be exact. I had just lost the home I had been sharing somewhat comfortably with my three siblings, my mom, my mom's boyfriend, Devon, and his son. I had just graduated from college the month before and was one month shy of my twenty-second birthday.

I never liked any of my mother's boyfriends because she had a knack for attracting guys who were fresh out of prison. You know, the ones who can't keep a job and don't want one for that matter. But this one I really could not stand. No matter how much my mother begged me to give him a chance, I just couldn't. It was hard to understand someone who couldn't keep a job, had multiple kids, and couldn't stay sober or drug-free through the night.

I'm a very sympathetic person, and I live for others to like me no matter how hard I must try; I'm weirdly built that way. But when your gut tells you something or someone is wrong, listen to it. Never wait for the fire to start.

As I said, my mother had a knack for picking terrible lovers, whether they were drug dealers, married, or alcoholics. She had them in her life, and she thought she was being a good mother by keeping most of them away from her children, but I always knew about them.

It was hard for my mom to hide a man who was coming out of her room in the middle of night when he and I both had the same idea to go to the bathroom—only *my* need to empty my bladder stemmed from drinking lots of liquid, not sex. Plus, my mom couldn't keep quiet to save her life during sex. I am a heavy sleeper, but the slightest movement or sound can quickly wake me out of a deep sleep. So, you can imagine that hearing my mother's sexual pleasures coming from the room next to mine was not so pleasant.

I couldn't sleep for hours after she was done with her monthly performance. Something inside kept me from closing my eyes, even after there was silence. There was something unsettling about knowing my mother just had sex with some man she barely knew, or knew for just the night, and it was even harder when I had to listen to their pleasures during the night.

It was difficult to make eye contact with her the next morning. I'd use blank facial expressions to avoid any sign that I knew of her midnight conquests. I didn't know much about sex back then, other than what I had seen watching porn. And before you judge, what teen didn't watch or come across porn at least once in their lives?

But because I didn't know too much about sex, I saw it as something dirty and stinky, judging from the smell coming from my mother's bedroom. Soon I was getting fairly good at hiding my facial expressions and keeping things that hurt me wrapped up inside. But how did my mother's bad choices in men and midnight pleasantries turn me into Bag Girl? To answer that, we must go back to the very beginning.

Chapter 2
The Black Kid

Born and raised in Martinsburg, West Virginia, in 1992, to a young mother who couldn't wait more than five months before conceiving a second time, I didn't have an ideal mother. She was young, naïve, and the opposite of mother of the year. I do not think being a mother was what she wanted. No, what she wanted was to be the life of the party. But, then again, becoming a mother at such a young age is not ideal for anyone—life of the party or not.

Be that as it may, my mother went out every night, leaving two kids at home who could not really fend for themselves. But I will say it amazed me how she had the strength to go out every night, come home first thing in the morning to shower, and head out to work an eight-to-twelve-hour shift. Some days, the only time we saw her was when she was getting ready for work, and we were getting ready to go to the babysitter or to spend a half-day at school, during those earlier years.

Since I was the oldest, I could not be weak. It was something I knew was expected of me to not show any signs of weakness around my mother because she didn't like crying. "Punk ass kids" was her preferred saying. Plus, I felt if I couldn't be strong for my siblings, then who else would be? I had to be strong for my brother. So, I quickly went from being a seven-year-old to the mother of a five-year-old, who was going on six. We moved to a trailer park, and I had to learn how to feed him and myself. Everything, at first, was microwaved. I had to learn how to get myself and my brother up and ready for the babysitter or school. Some days were easier than others, especially when my mother was there.

Before moving to that trailer park, I remember happier times. Like any child my age, I was active, went outside, and played with other kids. I was what my mother called "in a child's place." And although I was physically fit and healthy, I was slim. In fact, if you were to ask anyone in my family, they would tell you that I looked like I was starving. But after moving to our new home, I became chubby, unhealthy, and my hormones got the best of me.

I barely remember the first community my brother and I grew up in. We were there a while, but not long enough to create memories. With the exception of one other mixed-race family in the trailer park, we were the only Black family living there. And it wasn't long before the teasing and bullying started.

This, I remember.

The bullying and teasing made it easier for me to play mother to my two little brothers. Mom had just met her next one-night stand, and it turned into nearly a decade-long relationship. It was no surprise that she met him at a nightclub, and their one night together resulted in her pregnancy.

As soon as I got off the school bus, I would book it straight home just to avoid the angry mob of children who didn't like me because of my skin color. It was not easy being the only Black child in an all-white trailer park, and after I was diagnosed with diabetes and Polycystic Ovarian Syndrome (PCOS) at the age of eight, life there became even more unbearable.

How do you teach an eight-year-old how to shave their face because they are growing a beard and long sideburns? You do not, and as if that was not humiliating enough, I was starting to grow pubic hair. How can an eight-year-old act normal when she is not like all the other little girls her age?

I didn't know it just yet, but my body was slowly turning against me, making my life feel like hell as an eight-year-old little girl. Kids quickly began to notice that I was even more of a misfit. They didn't understand that I had a hormonal imbalance that made me grow hair on parts of my body that only boys should have.

I was also taller than the average girl my age, so when we went out to restaurants to eat dinner as a family, it was hard for the staff to believe my mother when she told them I was only eight years old at restaurants that let kids eat for free if they were under a certain age. Mom got into plenty of arguments, trying to defend my age and the constant stares I got from the other guests, trying to enjoy their meals with their families. The gawks I would get from the staff glued my ass and feet to the chairs because who'd want to get up from the table so the whole restaurant could see who my mother was talking about while yelling at the top of her lungs?

I don't know if the stares were out of pity or disgust, but it was something I was able to eventually ignore. The only restaurants we ever went to were buffets. It was the easiest and cheapest way for a young mother of three to feed her children when she didn't want to cook. We went to these buffets a lot, more Chinese-style buffets than American, mainly because we filled up faster on Chinese than American food.

Fast food was a big part of our lives because our mom was either too busy living her life, or she was fast asleep before work. All of Mom's jobs had her working overnights or twelve-hour shifts, so we barely saw her. Soon, we got used to not having her around. Waking up most mornings without her became easier. I knew what I had to do and did it.

Chapter 3
Ernesto

Mom's boyfriend, Ernesto, didn't have time to spend with two children he didn't father. Plus, it didn't help that he spoke little English and drank Coronas like a fish needing water to survive. She found him at her favorite night club, Lobos. It was the go-to place back in the nineties for American women to find illegal Spanish men, who needed a place to stay for the night or forever.

Like the others, I didn't like him. He was just one of many, but I didn't like him at all. I don't know if it was the fact that he didn't speak English and I couldn't understand him, or if it was the evil I felt coming from him. He was young when my mom met him. She was young too, but he was even younger.

Mom gave Ernesto his first child within a year, and because he was so young, he didn't know how to take care of a baby. Because of the bullies that made it unbearable for me to go outside and play, I quickly adapted to taking care of a newborn in addition to taking care of my brother, who was less than a year younger than me. Mom now had a partying partner, but even when they weren't partying, Ernesto was drinking. She didn't mind his partying when it was with her, but when he went out without her and returned in the morning, falling over furniture, that's where she drew the line.

Ernesto's partying soon became out of control. He enjoyed partying more than Mom did, and he drank to excess. Pretty soon, he started going out after work and during his days off and not returning till morning, which forced Mom to stay up worrying about him all through the night, making endless calls to see if someone knew where he was or if he'd been spotted at Lobos.

Although he understood little English, Ernesto knew when my mom was pissed about him not coming home. It eventually boiled down to him going straight to his aunt's house before coming home because she would cook up a concoction that sobered him up, thinking my mom would yell at him less if he walked in the house less drunk than usual.

Once my mom found his hiding spot after the club, there was nowhere for him to hide. His partying was more intense than hers, and she began to see what we saw when she was away. But it didn't stop his drinking. If he couldn't go out and party, he brought the party to himself, which meant all his friends, and loud music, were blasting until the morning.

You would think that as a mother of three, introducing your young children to constant drinking, smoking, and loud music would be more of a concern. But as long as Ernesto was home and in her sights, it didn't seem to matter what he did. And since my brother and I couldn't beat them, we would join them till the morning or till we dropped.

For a while, my brother and I had our mother back, and all the work of watching and feeding my siblings didn't fall on me. We were allowed to be around other adults without being told to go away, and the best part was that we had no specific bedtime. Besides, the adults liked it when my brother and I were around because that meant they didn't have to get up for a fresh beer from the fridge or another plate of food.

For a minute, my brother and I felt like adults. There was a party virtually every night, and almost every night we watched the sun come up. But the fun faded quickly for my mother, even though she finally had what she wanted. Ernesto no longer satisfied her. She wanted more out of her life and a new lover. Soon, she struck up another argument with Ernesto, this time concerning her new lover's constant need to party.

During the time she was actually being a mother, Mom was concerned about our safety and what we were being subjected to on a daily basis, but none of her concerns dawned upon Ernesto because we weren't his kids to begin with. He had one child, and the fact that his child witnessed his loud music and constant drunkenness didn't seem to faze him at all either. He was just like my mother in so many ways, and when she saw how we viewed her neglect towards us, it didn't please her.

She soon realized that she couldn't stop Ernesto's drinking and his constant need to party, so every week she'd kick him out, and he'd seek shelter from his friends. Every week he'd leave the trailer with a giant black trash bag or two and walk the miles to a friend's house or until one of them would pick him up on the side of the road.

I felt bad for Ernesto even though he didn't like me, and I didn't like him, but his absence only made things worse. Once again, everything fell back on me. Mom couldn't concentrate without having him there, and the kids needed to be bathed and fed, so I made sure my siblings had what they needed to survive. In the same way we'd watch him walk out that door every week, he'd walk back in like nothing had happened. Seven days was too long for Mom to wait for him to come back, so she'd drive across town to pick him up, and they'd start over like there was nothing broken between them.

Chapter 4
The Wedding

Ernesto and my mom did this dance for over a decade. They even got married when I was around twelve years old. I don't remember my exact age, but I know my mother had just given birth to my baby sister, her fourth and final child. There was now me and my younger brother, plus our youngest brother and sister by our stepdad. It was a day of wedded bliss and happiness. It was a day of endless tequila and Mexican food. My mother finally looked very happy. She had the wedding she'd dreamed of, and she was surrounded by all of her friends and family.

I was happy that she was happy. That night went on forever, and I thought it would never end. The requests to dance from his side of the family were endless. The party went on so long that children started to fall asleep where they dropped, but it didn't stop their mothers and fathers from partying, and it didn't stop the flow of tequila and Coronas. I even think someone went out and bought more just to keep the party going.

The sun had set, the empty boxes of Coronas were piled high in an old rusty trash can in the back, and the only people left on the dance floor were the groom and his friends. The women and children had called it quits, mainly because half of the women were wearing heels and couldn't keep up with the men anymore. Finally, the owner of the hall ordered the party to come to an end and return the hall to its original condition.

The music stopped and the party was over, but the damage was already done. There were still endless amounts of food and, surprisingly, beer to take home. Cleaning up the mess was only half the battle. Have you ever tried to tell a drunk Hispanic person that the party is over, and they must go home without him either swinging or throwing up on you from alcohol poisoning?

It wasn't an easy task to take on, especially for the women with children who wanted nothing more than to go home.

We were the last ones to leave. Once the last car had driven away and most of the food and alcohol were gone, we were left with the mess, which we decided to tackle the following day so Ernesto and Mom could relax on their wedding night. They couldn't afford a honeymoon, so they just enjoyed each other's company from the comfort of home.

The very next morning, we all got up extremely early to go back and clean the hall, but we didn't realize how hard we'd partied the night before until we faced the damage. Balloons, streamers, plates, and endless beer bottles were strewn everywhere. There was a mess not only inside but also outside with empty beer boxes and plates still full of food from the night before, although some food had been eaten by nearby animals.

The sun had just started to set by the time we took the last bag of trash out to the dumpster. We packed up the rest of the food, wedding cake, and children into my mom's minivan and headed home.

We arrived home just as the last rays of sun disappeared into the night, and the thought of unloading food and cake from the van after so many hours of cleaning was not pleasing. However, food and cake couldn't sit in the van overnight, so we unloaded my sleeping younger brother and sister into our new apartment where we'd recently moved after Mom found out she was pregnant again. When my sister was born, at first it was weird. (I used to tell people she and my youngest brother were my stepsiblings.) Some thought I had given birth to my sister because Mom was never around. Plus, my sister looks just like me, and I look just like Mom.

    We went up and down, up and down, and up and down once more. By the time we'd finished unloading the van, my calf muscles were on fire, mainly because the building we lived in had steps outside that led to more steps on the inside, and those led to our apartment.

    I envied my sleeping siblings at that point. If only I were a toddler. Looking at the pile of wedding supplies and food that cascaded over the kitchen table gave me anxiety at the thought of having to put that shit away. But my brother and I were saved. Ernesto and Mom decided to put away all the things that resembled their newly found love for each other.

    The first thing Mom put away was the top of their cake. She wrapped it in foil and stuck it in the back of the freezer for them to thaw and eat on their one-year anniversary. Next came the food. Oh my God, there was so much food left over that I thought I'd never eat another damn taco or tamale again in my life. There was some American food that my aunt and Nana had made for the occasion, but it was still outweighed by all the Mexican food.

    Once all the chaos was removed, the only thing left to do was relax. Since my brother and I both had TVs in our rooms, we left Mom and Ernesto to have the living room to themselves. It felt good to sleep in our beds that night because we had stayed with family to give Mom and Ernesto their privacy the night before. My mother was finally a happily married woman with a complete family.

    But not everything magical lasts forever.

The honeymoon phase between Mom and Ernesto was short-lived, and it wasn't long before the arguments started back up again, whether it was about how they should raise their kids or his constant drinking. The partying didn't stop though; people just ended up behind our apartment with coolers full of beer and a mini grill. However, this time, partying didn't just consist of Ernesto's friends; it also included our new neighborhood friends and my equally drunk uncle who couldn't say no to a beer and a plate of food.

Our new neighborhood was ghetto, but it wasn't as bad as the racist one where we lived before. I was now going back outside to play with kids my age and feeling like a child again. I was still bullied and beat up by the other kids, but this time I had backup. My childhood friend Olivia, whom I'd met in second grade, lived out there and was popular among the other children in the neighborhood. Anytime she was around, I didn't get picked on or beat up as much.

Although Olivia and I were close, her friends didn't like me at all. It wasn't because they found out I had hair growing in all the wrong places or the fact that I was overweight for my age; they just didn't like me. Some people don't really need a reason; they just decide they don't, and that's what I dealt with growing up in my childhood neighborhood.

I tried to spend every waking moment with Olivia when I wanted to be outside. It was sad, but it was the only way I could keep from getting bullied, even when walking to the bus stop, which was just a hundred feet away. I was still a target of those who didn't like me when they spotted me walking by myself. My bullies always found a reason to tease or intimidate me, and I was even a target for grown adults who had children themselves.

Chapter 5
Coming of Age

When I was thirteen, my mother gave me my last birthday party. She said I was old enough that I didn't need a party for every birthday. So, she got the keys to the empty apartment across the hall from us and turned it into my final surprise sweet thirteen. There were a handful of people who came, and my mom's adult friends brought their kids.

Olivia and her family were there, but they were the only ones I had invited. I knew in that moment that I should have been grateful for what my mother had given me, but it was hard to appreciate something so precious because I knew it was going to be my last. When I looked around the room, all I could see were the adults my mom had invited to help fill the space, and the only person I invited was not having any fun.

Finally, it was time for cake and gifts. Mom made my birthday cake at home, and it was her first attempt at baking one to save money instead of buying one. It was my favorite—red velvet with cream cheese icing. She made it a two-layer cake, but since it was her first time ever, it leaned to the side a little bit and was held together by two wooden sticks in the middle.

The cake was so dry that it tasted like I was eating cotton balls covered in cream cheese icing. Judging by the looks on the guests' faces, they were not pleased either. They couldn't even force down my mother's dry cake. This couldn't have been more humiliating. There I was with the one person who was there for me, who was no longer having fun, in room full of my mom's girlfriends with their children, and a cake that was beyond repair. Milk couldn't even save that dry-ass cake.

After enduring the earlier parts of the evening, all that was left to do was to open gifts. My mother's friends didn't even know what to get me since they didn't know me all that well. So, they got me little cheap things that I could use in my spare time. Olivia's mom gave me a CD of Usher, my favorite singer at the time. The gift was from both my friend and her mother, so either she didn't know what to get me either, or she didn't have the money to buy me a gift. Either way, I received one gift that I liked. I played that CD on repeat as often as I could, on a giant CD player that didn't even fit in my pocket. Somewhere along the way, like all good things, it came to an end. And I traded that giant CD player for a cell phone that I could now listen to music on, no matter where I went.

With cake and gifts done, it was time to pack up and put away the rest of the food and decorations. Olivia helped me take the food and gifts across the hall to our apartment, and after we'd finished, she asked if I wanted to go outside and hang out with her. I'm sure I made up some lame excuse to put away the food so I wouldn't have to go outside, and just like that, she was gone. I would have loved to go with Olivia, but I wasn't looking forward to the other children, who would have made an already stressful and humiliating thirteenth birthday more devastating and unsatisfying. I was sure Olivia was off to enjoy herself more than she had with me.

I put as much food as possible into the fridge, but not everything would fit, so I left what wouldn't go bad on the dining room table. I didn't know what else to do after that, so I got another plate of food, sat on the couch, and reached for the remote to see what was on TV. The couch had become my sacred ground since I stopped going outside due to bullying, and I had become the ultimate lazy person.

I had gained so much weight that I was no longer the skinny girl who people thought was starving.

By that time, I couldn't sit on the couch without a plate of food or something edible by my side. It became second nature to have food in my sight while watching TV. I needed food just like my siblings needed me to be their mother, and I had never felt so hopeless. At the age of thirteen, my life was just beginning, but I felt like I had nothing to give but my undivided attention to my siblings. So, that's what I did. I attended to my younger siblings.

I could hear the women across the hall still enjoying their time together. The official after-party for them was just getting started now that I was out of the way.

Between commercials and listening to the party across the hall, I sneaked peeks of the outside world. I watched the kids enjoy the fall weather while the sun was still at its highest in the sky. Wishing I could be popular or even liked in the neighborhood, I missed being outside. But since I had become a couch potato and a mother to my siblings, sadly the outside world didn't mean much to me anymore.

I was protecting myself from being bullied, but in reality, I was afraid to go outside and be a kid again. I not only endured being bullied by kids my age, but equally disturbing was the mistreatment by their parents too. Growing up, my mother always taught my brothers to never put their hands on a woman. Obviously, the boys who were beating me up were not taught the same thing by their mothers.

Every time I got beat up or into a fight, which was never initiated by me, my mother would always say, "Don't you bring your ass home crying." If I did, she would threaten to lock me outside until I learned how to fight. But I was a born lover, not a fighter. The truth is, I didn't know how to fight. It was a skill I couldn't quite master. But when I got into a fight, I tried my best to at least try and draw some blood because usually once a person bled, the fight was over, or at least the one bleeding was distracted long enough for the other person to get away. But I usually drew the short end of the stick. I was always bleeding and bruised up, but surprisingly, I never got a black eye or a broken bone.

The sun was setting, and as I sat there reflecting on the turn my life had taken, I could hear the party across the hall getting louder. Every now and then, the ladies would come over to grab more food or drinks. Each time someone came over, they asked me the same thing: How come you're not outside playing with your friends. Oh, if only they knew. I was not prepared to be beat up on my birthday.

In answer to their repeated question, I would tell them that I liked being inside and put my head down in embarrassment. They would quickly move on because they would suddenly remember that they were only there for one thing, and they'd return to the party across the hall once they found it. Once in a while, my mom would come over just to ask, "Why are you sitting here by yourself on your birthday watching TV when you could be outside with your friends?" She knew I didn't have any friends, but she also didn't want me sitting on her couch all day. But I didn't have anything productive to do that didn't involve me getting beat up or bullied, and that could at least wait until the next day.

People always say that you'll eventually outgrow your bullies, and they'll eventually lose interest in bullying you, but that wasn't the case for me. I grew up, but my bullies never did. They just followed me wherever I went.

Chapter 6
High School, Sex, and Drugs

High school is usually a big deal for a teenager, especially for a girl. She usually has best friends, and she starts to wear makeup and cooler, hipper clothes that she picks out herself for the first time. And although I was more than happy to attend a new school in a higher grade, it wasn't all it was cracked up to be—at least not for me.

I remember feeling so excited to start nineth grade. I stayed up all night deciding on the right outfit for the first day, how I would wear my hair, and what shoes went with which outfit. Growing up, in my house, we were a Reebok family. Every year for school, my mom would buy us one pair of white and one pair of black Reeboks. If we wore the white ones, they couldn't have any scuff marks or any type of wear and tear on them, or that would be the last pair of white shoes we ever saw. But telling a teenager not to mess up a good pair of white shoes is like giving a dog a bone and telling him not to eat it. It's damn near impossible, especially in an overly crowded high school.

Olivia and I had been in every school together since the second grade, but we went our separate ways in high school. Yet we remained friends. She went to Hedgesville, and I went to Martinsburg. Based on our addresses, we were both supposed to end up at Hedgesville, but I guess me going to a different high school was in the making anyway because my family moved late into my junior year. Mom had me transferred to South Middle School, which is directly across the street from Martinsburg, in an attempt to get me away from the bullies I'd been around since elementary school. Here's where I met Marty!

We went from living in a three-bedroom apartment to a four-bedroom (counting the attic) house that was down the street from the school, so I walked a half mile every morning with my new friend, Marty, who lived around the corner from me. Walking to school wasn't ideal in the summer or winter months, and no matter the season, I always felt like I needed another shower once I got to school. Being overweight, I was not used to such cardio. However, I went to summer school before my freshman year to avoid gym class.

Marty and I became the best of friends. He was the all-American dream boy: tall and slender with blue eyes and dark brown hair. I had the biggest crush on him in middle school, but the only issue was that Marty didn't like girls in that way. He was my diva! So, he became my best friend and shopping fashionista. He used to meet me halfway between his house and mine every morning so we could walk to school back then. School wasn't a far walk, but trying to keep up with Marty, who had long legs to go with his tall, slender body, was hard. I was two hundred pounds when I started my junior year, so I needed the exercise during those middle school and early high school years, and Marty gave it to me.

By junior year, I was fifty or so pounds heavier than I was before we moved, and Mom was no longer with Ernesto. They were still legally married, but they were living in two different countries. He went back to Mexico when my sister was still a toddler, and Mom couldn't stop falling into bed with random strangers. Granted, she did that enough when they were still living together because the being faithful part of her vows was hard to accept. She cheated the whole time they were together, and he couldn't stop drinking.

Now we were living in this new house, and I was in the attic. This was the part where Devon came in. I didn't like being at home when Mom was with Ernesto because of his loud music and constant drinking, but I *really* hated being home when Devon was there. There wasn't any loud music, but there was always a kitchen full of his friends drinking and smoking weed. I'd walk into the house from school, and the smell would instantly knock me over. I didn't know what my mom saw in him. I mean, he couldn't keep a job, he drank like a sailor, and he smoked weed like it was going out of style.

The funny thing is, when they first met at our old apartment, Devon gave Mom some sob story about how he was trying to change his life and not drink or smoke anymore. And, of course, Mom bought it. She made all of her girlfriends, who still smoked, go outside so he wouldn't be tempted to start again. Yeah… But, that sob story didn't last long before I came home to find him rolling a blunt.

I never liked Devon. I liked him about as much as I liked any of Mom's boyfriends, flings, or whatever you want to call them. (They were more flings than anything because she never saw them again.) There was always some reason she gave them as to why they couldn't see each other anymore. Either they were too sensitive, too weak, or wanted more kids of their own. But with Devon, Mom saw something in him that, to this day, I still don't understand.

Devon had been in jail or prison more times than he could probably count, and he had multiple children by multiple women. He wasn't a father nor a father-figure at all. The women he procreated with knew this from the start, but they still chose to produce a baby with him. Sadly, not all of them were thinking properly at the time of conception—or before.

While many of my mother's parenting and dating choices were questionable, Mom never introduced us to any of her boyfriends unless they were serious. She only brought them around for some late-night fun when she thought we were all sleeping, and then she'd send them on their merry way.

She couldn't have a serious relationship with anyone, even the ones who were true keepers. She had one great boyfriend who we all liked named Keith. He was a teddy bear at heart and a gentle giant in person. Keith made her happy, and she made him happy, but his mother couldn't get over the fact that she was never going to have grandchildren as long as he was with my mom. So, my mom let him go. She never told him the reason why; she just let him down easy, and he moved on. Last I heard, he moved to Pennsylvania, found a great girl, and had a baby girl with her.

Back then, I couldn't understand why Mom gave him up, but now I know how hard it was for her. It hurt her for a while to even talk about it with her girlfriends, but she quickly took care of those feelings when the sun went down with one of her midnight booty calls. That went on for a while—having sex with random men and some not-so-random men. It was a feeling and a sound I couldn't get used to, which continued to make it hard for me to look my own mother in the eye.

When she let Devon in, I knew something about him wasn't right. It wasn't just a feeling; it was the way he looked at me and my siblings with disgust. It was like he was saying, "I'm not here for you. I'm here for your mom." The way he talked to her made me feel very uneasy, too. He was demanding, and he used his strong, loud voice to make her jump to her feet. Mom catered to him like he was the child she never had.

Devon was six foot seven and close to three hundred pounds. He ordered my mother around like she was his servant, and he was her owner. Still, my mom spent more money to keep food in the fridge and freezer than she did on her kids because God forbid that man had to get a job, which he was sure to keep no longer than a week, with a lunch large enough for four people to share. I grew up watching her being controlled and abused by so many of her previous boyfriends, but back then, she only had two children to think about instead of four.

Now I wasn't the only one witnessing Mom being ordered around. My siblings were seeing it too, and they hated every moment of it as much as I did. They hated him, and there was nothing I could do about it. We patiently waited for Mom to recognize how he was mistreating her and how wrong he was for her, but it was like the more he treated her like a dog, the more she wanted him to throw her his bone. I was starting to see my mom's type and the reasons she got rid of so many boyfriends before him, but they weren't as ignorant or abusive as he.

I was no longer seeing my mother for who she really was. Now, under the watchful eye of my younger siblings, you'd think she'd be more aware of this. But Mom craved nothing more than Devon's undivided attention. She was blinded by love. Or was it lust? To me, it was really neglect. When it was just myself and my younger brother, we received enough of Mom's attention, so it didn't bother us at all when she wasn't around. We never realized how much attention she wanted from her man until we got older, and all the responsibilities fell on us.

Looking back, I guess this was her way of saying, *You're grown now. It's my turn to do what I want to do.* But we weren't grown, and we didn't have any idea what we were supposed to do. We couldn't be parents. I couldn't be a mother, but it was expected of me. I couldn't just live for me; I had to live for them.

My younger siblings saw it, but I don't think they realized how much they idolized me as a mother-figure in place of the woman who gave birth to them. With Devon around so much, it was evident that he wasn't going anywhere anytime soon. When Mom wasn't staying at his place, before they moved in together, he was staying at ours, cluttering our small apartment with all of his belongings and constantly moving our furniture around to fit his own.

It didn't seem like Mom noticed that he was also getting rid of her things just to fit more of his life into ours. As long as he was comfortable in her bed and fed six times a day, she was happy. But more of his life was rudely inserted into our three-bedroom apartment before we moved into the house, like him suddenly inviting his friends over without Mom's permission or him deciding he would start smoking weed and drinking alcohol again.

Funny, right?

Mom shunned most of her closest friends because they smoked or drank heavily, and she'd do anything to avoid stirring up old memories of Devon's past life. I wondered did he isolate her to make sure she didn't have anyone else to rely on when things went south. Usually, she was the one doing most of the shunning when it came to men and her children and friends, but now Devon had much more power than the one who usually held the marbles.

It was simple psychology, really. You put two dominant people up against each other…only they didn't collide like two ships in the night. No, they had something keeping them together. But after observing Mom for a while, one would notice that more had changed than just her neglect of us; it was the fact that she couldn't control him. So, when he would leave for long periods of the day, her attitude would change towards us since we were the easier targets. On top of her diagnosis of bipolar depression, having him around was the only drug she needed. He kept her calm, sated, and everywhere but home.

When Devon wasn't there, calling him wasn't an option because Mom didn't want to come off as needy. For a woman with four children, she had no reason to be needy since she had us, but we didn't really have her... She was single. My older brother and I used to crave being left alone by our mother because those lessons taught us to make sure certain things were done after school and before bed, and they came in handy. For example, we would make sure there were no dishes in the sink or else she would wake us up in the middle of the night, even on a school night, to wash them. We made sure some type of meat was taken out of the freezer after we got home from school, or we would end up going hungry, or she would yell at us for making her buy takeout when she was low on money and there was food at home. Those types of moments taught us life lessons.

Devon seemed to be our biggest life lesson. Not only did it seem like he was never going anywhere and was inserting more of his life into ours, but our family of five (Mom included) also quickly turned into a family of eight. There was no surprise that a man of his status had a hard time keeping his own family together, so two—not one, but TWO—of his sons were sent to live with him, and when I say *him*, I mean *us*. Why? Because their mother was afraid and didn't know how to control them. Plus, they lived in a bad part of Washington, DC, so to keep them alive and out of trouble, she sent them to Devon.

This was laughable by all standards, seeing that the woman who was supposed to be their mother couldn't control her own children, so she sent them to live with someone who was less than a man and whose methods of fathering consisted of yelling. As long as his sons weren't in his way or cramping his style, he didn't care where they wound up.

I was starting to see the attraction between him and my mother for what it was. They were, in some ways, just alike. But being told on short notice that his two children were coming to live with us when we already had little to no space boiled my mother's blood. When they finally arrived, they were hardly children. One, of whom his mother was most afraid, was my youngest brother's age and had a terrible no-can-do attitude. The one who was my age had already been in jail at least once and sadly resembled every bit of his father, inside and out.

Because I'm my mother's daughter, I also inherited her strong resting bitch face (RBF), so when they came, I didn't know how to turn my RBF off. They knew it, but because they are their father's sons, they didn't care or have time for it.

I was never one to ignore what was there, no matter how hard I tried, but my brothers eventually got used to them being around. I, on the other hand, prayed they wouldn't be there—not even a trace—before walking through the door after school.

Going home after school was more of a letdown than being in school with the same bullies I grew up with. The one my age—oh, let's just call him Devon Jr.—was literally every bit of his father. Because he was older, he was allowed to behave just like Devon in almost every way. "Like father, like son," they say.

Chapter 7
A Father's Love

If eight people in a small apartment isn't enough, let's throw in one more and make it nine. Just when we were getting into a routine of having to step over the other two, along came the youngest one. Let's call her Raven.

Raven was the youngest and last of all Devon's children; she was barely two years old. He'd procreated with her drug-addicted mother, apparently back when crack was more important than she and Raven was. Fortunately for Raven, she didn't have her mother's wits or half the mind her father had. It was hard to believe she came from either of them because she was the chunkiest, most adorable thing you'd ever lay eyes on. And God, she loved her father. A daughter craves her father's love, and because she was so young, that was what she wanted most.

Like me, Raven didn't know her father; although, she did know who he was. I thought one person was my father until my mother casually told me one day who he really was after he was released from prison. Mom asked me if I wanted to go to Walmart with her, which was rare, and they ambushed me in the music section. I didn't really care for it and walked away, so Mom got his number for me just in case I changed my mind about meeting him. I didn't. A year or so after he was released from prison, he ended up overdosing. I never really got the chance to get to know him.

But at that age, children don't know very much, so when she thought she was doing something good, it was really something to tick him off, which didn't take much.

I hated when Devon spanked Raven. He was a big man with big everything, including hands, and her body was so small. She didn't mean to do anything wrong, but because she was a child, it didn't take much to piss off an alcohol and drug addict. Now, I'm not saying that he laid into her but imagine someone as big as Shaq spanking the average two-year-old. It didn't look pleasant, but she wasn't my child, so I didn't have a say-so, nor was it any of my business.

I just knew Raven kept wanting to come back to see her daddy when it was his week to have her, like any good child, and I didn't mind having her around most of those times. Pretty soon that three-bedroom apartment just couldn't hold all of us anymore, so we moved. The new house even came complete with a full-size basement in addition to the attic, which ended up being my room because my mother thought I would want my privacy.

I had to go through my sister's bedroom just to get to my room and the bathroom, but luckily for me, the attic was renovated before we moved in. The problem was more the old rusty stairs and the fact that I had to pass through two bedrooms when I wanted to shower, but it was our first house ever, and I was proud that we finally had taken a step up in the world.

I felt like a normal person for once. I thought that having a house meant we had some type of money because we'd lived in apartments and trailers for as long as I could remember. It was almost embarrassing because everyone I knew had a house, and it wasn't a small, dainty house either—it was a *house*. So when we moved into this one, I felt some sort of joy. In hindsight, I guess I was happy that I lived right down the street from my best friend, Marty, and around the corner from school. Marty made all the difference because he was always full of life and had the coolest hippy of a mother. He also liked to take photos, so I was always his model. We confided in each other, and I was always learning about his new love interests.

For a moment there, I was actually happy. We had a house, and I had my closest friends—Marty and Olivia. But all good things must come to an end. No matter how hard Mom tried to be patient with Devon, things just weren't working out. But she knew how to put on fake impressions for her friends.

Devon was having a hard time with Raven's mom. She would go through periods of screaming at him when she was either using again or going through withdrawal, making it harder for him to be around and giving Raven the short end of the stick. On top of that, he couldn't keep a job because he didn't do well when it came to being told what to do. He definitely had his share of problems with authority. That put all the responsibility on Mom to make ends meet by working more than one job, which meant she was never home, as usual. And it put more pressure on me to make sure everyone was fed and had a bath at night when Mom and Devon weren't there. Devon's absence pissed Mom off more because she would call looking for him, and when she couldn't reach him on his cell, she would blow up mine just to see if he was actually home or just ignoring her.

Honestly, we barely saw either of them—Mom because she had to work twice as hard just to make sure the lights stayed on and food was in the house and Devon because he didn't have to be there. So, if you felt bad for me before for having to play Mom to my own three siblings, add Devon's two-year-old to the mix.

Devon would wait almost an hour after Mom had left for work before he would come trampling up to my room to inform me that he was going out and ask if I could watch Raven. But he wasn't really asking; that was his way of *telling* me to watch her. I'd roll my eyes, sigh, and look away, and that was his signal to leave. I mean, who else was going to watch a two-year-old? Not my little sister, who was once the baby in the family. When I told my mom, she did not care; she only cared if he was home, and she became frustrated when he was not.

I'd do my usual when both adults were away. I'd turn down my TV and listen for shit that didn't sound right or for something they weren't supposed to be doing. They were almost never quiet, so I knew I had time before screaming started or something broke and my name would be yelled. When it got too quiet, that usually meant they were asleep or settled down to play video games.

The older they got, the easier my job as babysitter became. All I had to do was cook and make sure baths were done. But being Devon's keeper, as my mother thought, didn't make my job easier. When Devon and my mom were home together, they hardly spent time with each other, so why did it bother my mother so much when he wasn't there? Maybe it had something to do with the fact that he used to be a drug addict or that he had way too many baby mamas for one person. Either way, my mother was never at ease unless she knew exactly where he was at all times, and that usually meant using me as her investigator, which was funny because there used to be a time when my mother never wanted me in her business and told me to stay in a child's place. Now, here she was dragging me out of "my place" and into "her business." But now I was not only babysitting his children, but I also had to play Inspector Gadget with him.

Chapter 8
The Game Plan

With my junior year under wraps, I could only see freedom in my sights. I craved nothing more than to be out of my mom's house and into my own, but the more I thought about it, the more flustered I became over the fact that no one would be around to protect my younger siblings. I couldn't care less about Devon's kids because they were his problem, but Raven was a whole different breed. She was the annoying two-year-old, who wanted nothing more than her daddy's love and affection.

I tried not to think too much about leaving this place and how hard it would be, and I focused on how my future would shape up once I got out into the world and ventured on my own. I wanted to be free of the lifelong battle of being someone's mother, nurse, cook, and chauffeur, yet I had anxiety about what would happen next.

What the hell is wrong with me? I thought. *I've been trapped in this life of horror for years, and when it's finally coming to end, I almost don't want it to.*

I didn't know where I was going; all I knew was that I wanted to be nothing like my mother. I was going to be better than her. But my anxiety about the future was mine and mine alone to deal with. My mother had her own problems, and since we didn't really have a good mother-daughter relationship, it wasn't like I could go to her with my problems. She was too busy trying to figure out how she could keep Devon in the house when she was working during all hours of the day to provide for us, but it would take more than just her wits to keep him grounded.

So, since Devon liked to cut hair (which was how he met my mom), the plan was to give him his own barber shop inside the house. The two-story house had plenty of space for raising a family of four with a few extra on the side, but there definitely wasn't enough room to open a full barber shop. My mother was reluctant at first, but she was willing to do anything to keep her man. So, they found someone to give him an old, but still-in-good-shape, barber chair. He already had a full-size mirror and clippers, so he just needed that final piece for his shop.

If Devon wasn't good for anything else, he was good for a haircut. My mom's best friend owned a salon and often employed her when she wasn't working a fulltime job. Mom did hair, but she didn't know how to cut. So, Devon was hired to service the male clients. Mom was a stylist, and Devon was a barber.

Still, socially awkward, I didn't like to be around a lot of people or become the center of attention in any situation, but I realized that a barber shop in our home meant some degree of interaction with others would be unavoidable. It was bad enough that I had to deal with Devon's three kids the majority of the time, so coming home from school became a slower trip than usual.

I'd take my time walking home, enjoying the quiet peace around me, watching cars drive past me, some in a hurry and some not rushing at all. Then I'd get to the corner where my house stood, and I'd take a deep breath because the worst was yet to come. I'd slowly walk down the hill towards the crosswalk that led to my side of the street.

By contrast, walking to school every morning was always a race against the clock because I was either late getting up, or I was delayed because someone was hogging the bathroom. And the worst part was that we had *two* bathrooms.

But on my way home from school, before I'd even make it up the hill that led to my house, I'd instantly find myself looking for my mom's car. If she was home, at least some part of me had relief. But on days she wasn't there, I already knew my game plan before I walked inside that door: *Don't make eye contact, head straight upstairs to my room, and stay there until I hear Mom's voice.* Ironically, I still look for my mother to help relieve my anxiety in social situations, even though she wasn't there to help me throughout my life when I needed her most.

As I approached the house, I could hear the riot that was coming from inside. I rolled my eyes in annoyance and took the six steps to our door. I dug into my Thirty-One purse for my house key while growing more and more annoyed by the noise coming from inside.

Once I found my key, I shoved it into the keyhole and twisted it while turning the doorknob at the same time. I made quick due with removing the key from the keyhole, only to look and see one guy bobbing back and forth in front of another whose feet I could only see, alerting me that he was sitting down in the chair while having his hair cut. They seemed to be having a grand old time, not even realizing that I'd just walked in and slammed the door shut.

I threw my key back into my bag and started power walking past the man who was still bobbing his body back and forth in an effort to put on a show. Devon had his music blasting, and it grew louder as I walked past. None of them looked up or even noticed that I'd just flown past them in an effort to avoid them. The smell of alcohol and weed was in the air, and I knew that was one of the reasons they weren't paying me no mind. And for once, I wasn't even bothered by the fact that Devon was doing what he promised Mom he wouldn't, which was smoke in the house or around us since my younger brother had chronic asthma.

I was sure Mom would smell it when she decided to come home, but a part of me didn't even care because it wasn't like she was going to say or do anything about it. After all, she got what she wanted, and that was to have Devon at home.

I could hear faint mumbling on my way up the stairs, but I couldn't make out what they were saying because the music was too loud. It almost made my anxiety rise, but I tried to ignore it and kept it moving up to my room.

Once I was up the stairs, I made it a point to stop and check on my brothers to see if they were home and what they were doing. I opened the door to their room and saw them, yelling and shouting at whomever was on the other end of that receiver, in full-on game mode. A faint smile crept across my face, and without them missing a beat, they said in unison, "*Hi,* Toza." Then they continued playing with their game without even looking up.

I closed the door and turned to my left to open my sister's bedroom door, which also led to my room up in the attic. She was watching TV on the bed with Raven. They both looked up at the same time and greeted me as I turned to close the door behind me. I said, "Hi," in response and reached for my doorknob when my sister asked if I knew where Mom was. I replied, "No," while opening the door to my room and stepping inside.

The noise from downstairs was a near faint sound as I walked the twelve steps up to my room. I looked around my room and felt the relief of being in my own sanctuary and away from the chaos that was happening just a few feet below me. Tossing my purse and drawstring backpack onto my bed, I looked around my room for the remote to my TV. The TV almost immediately burst to life with a loud pop. My TV was old, so every time I turned it on, it made a loud popping sound, sometimes startling me because I never knew when it was going to happen.

Nothing of interest was on the first channel, so I sat down on my bed and reached down to take my shoes and socks off and relieve some of the pressure of wearing shoes. My shoes were not too small or too tight; I just hated wearing them all day. Once my shoes were off, I wondered if it was too early to take off my pants and really get into that relaxing stage, but I knew the moment I did, I'd be forced to go downstairs and retrieve something from either the kitchen or the living room, which would require me to walk briskly past Devon and his loud, obnoxious friends yet again.

God! Where are you, Mom? I thought.

I decided to unbutton my pants, releasing my gut from their hold, and slide my zipper down just far enough for more comfort. I was careful not to unzip them too far because if I did, they'd fall down when I got up to stand, which would force me to button them up again just to restart the process of unzipping them halfway. Unsatisfied by the school lunch, I was starting to get hungry again, and the thought of going back downstairs to see what was in the fridge did not appeal to me. I was really hating my mother for not being there.

I was nestled in my bed, watching whatever I could find of interest on TV. The chaos of Devon and his friends was still happening beneath me, and I constantly heard the front door slam shut. With each slam, my bedroom and my bed rattled.

Boy, this house must be really old, or *I'm in the unsafe part of the house*, I thought.

It sounded like more and more of Devon's friends had now invaded our home because the commentary kept growing louder and louder. I rolled my eyes in exasperation and let out a loud sigh at the thought of them being so damn loud instead of just turning down the music so they could all hear each other. I knew for a fact that once my mom arrived, all that shit would come to an end, but I didn't know if she was working today or not because I'd lost track of her work schedule. Plus, it wasn't like I could just ask her. She hated it when one of us, mostly me, asked if she was at work. So, I'd just have to suck it up until she came home. The kids hadn't told me they were hungry yet, so I figured that bought me more time before the complaints started coming.

    I kept looking at my phone to see how late it was, and each time I looked, I was more and more disappointed. It was only 3:34 p.m. I hadn't been home from school that long, but it seemed like an eternity since I'd walked through that door. I was getting tired, but my body wouldn't let me wind down. I was almost afraid to close my eyes because the only thing between me and a potential intruder was an old fitted sheet from my bed. That thought alone left me uneasy, and even today, whenever I hear someone's feet coming up my stairs, it still startles me.

    I always knew when Devon was coming up here because he'd stomped and grunt at the same time because his old-ass body had been through God-knows-what. My siblings, mainly my brothers, liked to skip every other step, letting me know it was one of them, and my sister would just yell from the door downstairs that divided my room from hers.

    But I'd always been nervous around people I didn't know, not saying that Devon would allow any of his friends to come up to my room because they'd have no reason to. I just didn't like the feeling of uneasiness. Growing up, Mom used to bring people over so the party could continue at home—more men than women. The only women she'd bring home from a night out were her two closest friends, who also had kids around my age.

When our moms wanted to go out, which was just about every day or every weekend, all of us eldest girls would band together and watch our siblings so none of us were ever alone. I think it was the cheapest way out when our mothers didn't want to pay for a babysitter.

So, it wasn't like I wasn't around strange men all the time, but something changed in me. Something left me bitter and uncomfortable around unfamiliar people, especially men. Was I wrong for feeling the way I did about strange men, or was I just paranoid? Either way, I wasn't really comfortable around Devon's friends to begin with, and it's not like any of them were saints or gentlemen around women. They were all dogs, and they treated women more like property than like people. Just listening to some of their conversations when I was nearby made me sick. I would say it was no surprise they were single, but they took pride in being single and having sex with whomever came their way. Hearing Devon agree with his friends made me wonder what my mother saw in him and whether she'd agree with him if she heard the words coming out of his mouth.

I was fighting sleep, here and there, but I allowed myself to close my eyes just for a moment to reboot, although I was still aware of my surroundings. I was listening carefully like a canine, waiting for its master to walk by. Between the ruckus below, I could hear Raven's little laughs, and it made me smile inwardly. I loved hearing her little laugh. It was so angelic and calming. She and my sister must've been watching something funny because her laughter continued.

I could almost ignore what I was hearing three floors below me, just almost. Pretty soon, I couldn't hear anything at all. I felt my body relax into the mattress. I was getting comfortable—too comfortable. I slipped into a deep sleep, and pretty soon I was dreaming… Dreaming about life outside this life. My brain wouldn't shut off because I soon realized that I'd fallen asleep, so I awoke abruptly like someone was there standing over me.

I opened my eyes widely, trying to adjust to the light even though it was still daylight out. My heart pounded hard as if someone were just chasing me. I stared at the TV in an attempt to find something that would grab my attention, but I could feel my eyelids getting heavier, and they were slowly shutting again.

Wow, I can't believe I'm this tired. I woke up at my usual time this morning for school and made it through all of my classes just fine. But I've gotten to the point in my life where I actually want *to take a nap. Boy, I'm getting old, but unfortunately, my body won't let me settle into the deep abyss of slumber. It knows I'm not really comfortable enough to, and my anxiety is making me feel as if I don't deserve it.*

I sleepily checked the time again on my phone. It still hadn't been that long since I'd last checked it. My phone said that it was six minutes till 4:00 p.m., and yet, my mother was still not home. *Where in the hell could she be?* I hadn't been home for a full two hours yet, but I was starving, and the only thing that kept me in my room was the fact that I was exhausted, and no one had come up to tell me they were hungry.

The party downstairs didn't seem like it was coming to an end anytime soon, and I didn't know what to do about food. I was used to going hungry, but I couldn't let my siblings go hungry. As long as my brothers were invested in their game and my sister was cool with watching TV with Raven, I had nothing to worry about. Eventually,

Mom would walk through that door, hopefully with food in her hands.

I yawned and blinked as tears of exhaustion escaped both sides of my eyes. I tried to wipe them away, blinking hard once or twice, trying to regain my vision once more. I looked up at the fitted bed sheets that covered the empty space where a door should be and noticed that it was swaying back and forth. My air conditioner was not on, and my window was shut, so I wondered why my sheet was moving.

I was so tired that I thought it might be a ghost of some sort, and my imagination was playing mind games on me. So, I tucked my right hand under my pillow and my left hand between my thighs and nestled into my bed once more, feeling the comfort of lying down. This bed was as old as me, and it was still comfortable. My grandfather bought it for me back when I was in middle school. It was my first real big-girl bed; at least to me it was because when I rolled, I didn't hit the floor. After all those years, it was still the most comfortable thing I'd ever lay on. I planned on taking this bed with me when I finally moved out because at least I could still pass it off as new. *And it would be the first step in my having furniture in my own place*, I thought as the deep ecstasy of sleep hit me again. *I must stay awake. I must stay awake*, I repeated to myself, but the strength to stay awake was getting harder with each passing moment.

"What the hell was that?" I jolted awake from the slam of the door. *Shit. I fell asleep again. For how long this time?* I wondered.

I heard something—that voice. I tried to focus on what I was hearing, but I was still a little drowsy from my brief nap. It was my mother. She was finally here. I rolled over and looked outside. There was still daylight out, so it couldn't be that late. I rolled back over to check the time on my phone and noticed that it was ten minutes after five. I'd slept a whole hour, but it didn't even feel like I'd slept at all.

Mom was yelling about something, but I couldn't make out what. I could hear my sister and Raven run down the stairs after her. They too must've been relieved that she was finally home.

I could hear Mom yelling for them to get out of the kitchen so she could make dinner. As soon as she said that, my sister asked, "What's for dinner?"

"You'll find out when I put it on your plate." Classic Mom. I'd heard that response a lot growing up, so it was nice to hear it being said to someone else for a change.

I started to doze off again because it was much easier now that Mom was here, so I quickly rolled over to get comfortable and felt a sensation that made me jump up. I couldn't remember the last time I went to the bathroom. I loved having privacy, but the worst part about living on the very top floor was that I had to go down one floor just to pray that no one was in the second-floor bathroom.

I lay there a little while longer, hoping to ignore the fact that I really had to go to the bathroom, but after a few minutes of realizing that it was getting worse, I made the decision to go downstairs. I planted my feet onto the floor and slowly rose, giving my body the chance to catch up with the rest of me before taking a step towards the exit.

I sleepily walked the twelve steps down to my sister's room and stumbled out into the hallway. I was surprised to see the bathroom door wide open, letting me know that it was unoccupied. I quickly made my way into the bathroom, nearly missing the toilet from exhaustion. Once I was in place, I got a whiff of what Mom was cooking.

Hmm, I thought, *whatever she's making smells really good.*

I could usually tell what she was making just by the smell of it because our meals never changed when Mom made dinner. When she wanted to make a quick dinner to feed a whole village, she went for spaghetti, and when she felt like she had all the time in the world, it was usually something fried or Salisbury steak with mashed potatoes and corn on the side. But this smell, I couldn't pinpoint. I couldn't tell if it was something fried or something she threw into the oven. Whatever it was, I knew it was going to be good.

Nana, my mother, and I were pretty good cooks. We all learned to cook early, and we learned it from the best. Well, some of us learned early. According to my grandfather, it was a while before Nana learned how to cook a good, decent meal that he actually wanted to eat.

After I was done using the bathroom, I decided to sit there for a little while, relishing in the sweet smell of dinner. When I decided that I'd sat there long enough, I got up and turned on the hot water in the sink. I looked in the mirror and noticed how rough I looked even though I hadn't even slept that long. My ponytail was now sideways, hair that was once brushed back was now standing up all over my head, and my face looked like I'd slept hard all night.

I ran my hands under the hot water, washed them, and reached for my washcloth that was hanging in the shower behind me to wash the sleep off my face. I grabbed my brush from the linen closet and quickly ran it under the hot water and gently applied the bristles to my scalp to tame stray hairs. I turned off the hot water and headed out of the bathroom when I noticed that my sister and Raven were not in their room.

Hmm. They must still be downstairs with Mom. I thought about joining them downstairs just to be nosy and see what Mom was making for dinner until I heard the nuisance of Devon's friends. *Great. They're still here. I think I'll pass on going downstairs until Mom calls for dinner.*

Thinking I was going to nap a little longer until dinner was ready, I headed back upstairs to my room. But now I was restless and couldn't even think about closing my eyes. So, I found something good to watch on TV and then ignored it by picking up my phone to search through social media to see what was going on in the world. It seemed like everyone I went to school with had a life outside of school, except for me.

What the hell is wrong with me? Every post is of someone doing something great and entertaining with their life, and here I am being the weirdo, liking every post because I have nothing better to do.

The aroma of what Mom was cooking was quickly filling the house because it had now reached the third floor and was distracting me from my boring life. I commented on people's pictures here and there, hoping to strike up a conversation so someone would talk to me. I honestly didn't even know why I had a phone. No one ever called it or texted me unless it was my mom or siblings in need of something.

An hour went by, and my phone went off. "Ooh, a text message! Oh, wait. It's just Mom, telling me that dinner is done. Great," I mumbled to myself, "now I get the pleasure of going downstairs and facing Devon's friends."

The music was still playing loudly, but I didn't hear much commotion, so when I finally made it down to the first floor, I peeked around the corner to see if someone was there. Nope, it was just Devon standing in the full-size mirror, brushing his own hair. I guess the party was over.

I slid the rest of my body down the last of the stairs and briefly walked past Devon, but he saw me in the reflection and said, "Hey, Toza."

Without turning around or missing a beat, I said, "*Hi, Devon*," using my tone to let him know that I wasn't interested in conversing with him. I power-walked my way into the kitchen.

He knew I had no interest in talking to him, so he talked to me in a cocky way just to annoy me. It looked like I was late getting downstairs because all of my siblings were already at the table eating their dinner, and Mom was standing over the stove making a big-ass plate, likely for Devon since he was the only one who would eat for six people.

"Tacos! My favorite." Now I had to decide if I wanted to make a taco salad or pull out the tortillas and make individual tacos, which was time consuming but still just as good as a taco salad. Looking at my choices and my siblings' sloppy plates, I opted for a salad.

Mom looked up from the stove to say hi and then asked how my day went at school. I spouted my usual short piece and kept it moving towards the bag of tortilla chips. It looked like I was the only one who went for a taco salad because I was first to open the bag. Mom heard me opening it and told me to leave it open because she wanted to make a salad too.

I did as I was told and headed over to the stove where she'd just finished making Devon's plate. I was one to make my food look pretty even though I knew it was going to look like a disaster in the end. But that still didn't stop me from making my taco salad look like it belonged in a

Home and Garden magazine. I then sat down and scanned my bowl for where I should start first.

In the same way I was last to come downstairs, I was also last to leave the table. The boys had seconds and even Devon had already come in once for his seconds, not that he needed it. I sat there contemplating whether I was still hungry enough to go for seconds or if I could pass it up and be comfortable for the rest of the night. It wasn't a decision to make lightly because these extras wouldn't be there for long between Devon and my brothers. So, I opted to have seconds, but this time, I decided to go for two soft tacos instead.

With a satisfying meal and a full belly, I headed back up to the third floor. Once I was back in my room, I contemplated taking my shower now before the boys or letting my belly rest first. I sat on the edge of my bed while weighing my options. My deep thoughts took a little longer than expected, but after about half an hour, I decided to grab my towel and head down for a shower.

But I'd waited too long.

When I got down to the second floor, the smell of flowers was in the air, and I knew for sure that it was my sister. She had her music playing from her little hand-held speaker, and I knew it was going to be a while. So, I turned right around and headed back upstairs, kicking myself in the ass for waiting so long but also challenging myself to head downstairs the moment she got out so no one else had the chance to go before me again.

Once I'd returned to my room, I plopped down onto my bed. I was grateful because as old as the bed was, it still held against my weight. I laid down, looked up at the ceiling, and felt the full weight of what I'd just eaten come crashing down on me. I really shouldn't have had seconds. As I turned onto my side to relieve some of the pressure, I raised up on my elbow and immediately looked down. But as I bowed my head, my chin hit my boobs, stopping me in my tracks. I had to push my chest in just so I could sneak a peek at my increasingly growing gut, which was literally lying on the bed.

"God, this is not sexy at all. I really need to lose my gut," I said to myself. "No man is going to want me as long as my own gut is lying on the bed."

I'd never been this big, and I couldn't remember the last time I was skinny or what it felt like to be skinny. The thought depressed me because my high school years were just about over, and I'd never had a boyfriend or had ever been asked out.

"No wonder. Look at me. I look disgusting, and I feel disgusting." I promised myself to start eating lighter meals and to exercise more than five days a week.

Then a thought crossed my mind. *I walk to school five days a week. I bet if I truly eat less and stick to this diet, I'll actually be skinnier by the time I graduate next May.*

I made this promise to myself and listened for the shower. There was so much noise between my TV, Raven's constant laughing at whatever was on her TV, and my brothers cussing at the game. So, I headed back downstairs to see if my sister was actually still in the shower. Sadly, she was. At this point, I had no idea what the hell she was still doing in there. She weighed about fifty pounds, soaking wet, and had much less than I did to wash, so what the hell was she doing? The smell of flowers was now faint, so I assumed she was in there just standing under the spray of hot water. But there were seven of us who still needed to shower, and the water heater was only so big.

Luckily, Devon's two boys went back home for the weekend to visit their mother, so that was two less people who needed a shower. But, at this rate, there wouldn't be any hot water left.

I decided to go into her room and wait for her to get out of the shower. I refused to walk up those damn stairs again.

As soon as I sat down on the bed, Raven looked up and said in the cutest voice, "What are you doing in here? This is Rika's room, not your room."

I said, "I know, but I'm waiting for Rika to get out of the shower so I can get in."

"Oh," she replied and then lay back down to continue watching TV.

She was watching *Phineas and Ferb*, my favorite Disney Channel TV show. Now I understood why she was laughing so hard; the show was quite funny and super cute. I was focused on the show when my sister appeared, dripping wet from head to toe, glaring at me hard for sitting on her bed and for being in her room. Before she could say anything, I was up and on my way to the bathroom, which was steamy from all the heat, giving the air a damp feeling.

I turned on the water and ran my hand under the stream. I was grateful that it was still hot. I turned on the shower and jumped in. I quickly wet my body before reaching for my body wash. The top felt a little light, so my guess was someone had been using my body wash. I rolled my eyes at the thought of never being able to have anything to myself without someone else helping themselves to it.

I made quick with my shower since I didn't have to wash my hair like my sister, and I was out in less than ten minutes. Patting myself on the back for leaving hot water for the next person, I grabbed my towel, wrapped it around my body, and before totally stepping into the hallway, I made sure no boys were out there. I hated the feel of my wet, damp feet touching the bare floor, so I literally got my cardio every day just running from the bathroom to my fully carpeted room. Plus, Mom hated when we got out of the shower with wet feet and tracked water everywhere.

Once I was back in my room, I was winded from trying to save my feet from getting dirty all over again. I dropped my towel and immediately started drying my feet and the rest of my body in an effort to quickly get dressed because my bed looked a little lonely. I hung up my towel to dry for tomorrow's shower, marched back over to my bed, and planted myself right in the middle of the mattress for warmth and comfort.

It didn't take me long to get comfortable. Going to bed had always been my favorite part of the day. You know how some people say, *There's no place like home?* Well, I've always said, *There's no place like bed.* It was my place of comfort and peace. I would catch an attitude when I had to get out of bed for school because the thought of losing that perfectly warm spot was just maddening.

There was still a sliver of light outside, but most of it had been lost. I decided to turn off my lamp on the nightstand as the last few rays of light peeked through my curtains. The rest of my room was a little dark, giving it a relaxed feel to help set my mind at ease.

I watched the Cooking Channel, which I'd always enjoyed but knew I shouldn't do as much when I had my mind set on losing weight before graduation. But when there was nothing else on, it was my go-to when I was settling down for the night. The good thing about being on the third floor was that no matter how hard I wanted a snack, you wouldn't catch me walking down three flights of stairs just to get one. So, I was half-watching TV and half-scrolling through my phone, but there were no replies on the comments that I'd left on people's pictures.

I took this as a sign to plug my phone into the charger and turn my focus to the TV. Besides, I figured it might give me an idea of what I would like to make one day for dinner. I was halfway through the show when I decided to roll over onto my right side, put my right hand under my pillow, and slide my left hand between my thighs. Then I closed my eyes and listened to the TV, allowing myself to visualize what was being made.

I must have dozed off, because when I woke up, a whole new cooking show was on. I turned off the TV and rolled over onto my stomach, which was my favorite position for when I really wanted to get comfortable and sleep well. Once my TV was off, I could hear the laughter of Raven and my sister below me.

"God! Why are they still up?" That girl could stay awake all hours of the night, and since my sister still rode the bus to school, she typically stayed up longer than the rest of us. She usually styled her hair for the next day, so the smell of burnt hair was about to be in the air from her over-straightening it.

And my brothers, I didn't know how they did it. They were usually up till 3:00 a.m., still playing their game, but they were never late for school. As the eldest, I needed my damn beauty sleep, so it didn't take long before I was in a deep slumber and didn't hear a thing around me.   Did I mention the main reason I hated being on the third floor was the location of the bathroom?

I was once again in a deep sleep when I rolled over, and my stomach pushed against my overly full bladder, making me immediately wake from sleep. I groaned at the thought of having to go to the bathroom this late, and I reached over and grabbed my phone to check the time. To my surprise, it was only 10:30 p.m. I'd only been asleep for less than three hours, and it felt like I'd been asleep all night. The last of the sun was miles away, and sheer darkness had settled in. I put on my slippers (I always forgot when it was time to shower), and stumbled over to the doorway, sleepily reaching for the hall light so I could make my way down the stairs without breaking my neck. Halfway down, I could see my sister's bedroom light was on, and Raven was still awake, judging by the conversation she was having with my sister.

I opened the door that divided our rooms, and to no surprise, my sister had everything laid out for doing her hair. She was straightening away when she briefly stopped to look up at me as I shielded my eyes from the bright light. I felt like a bear coming out of hibernation just to walk to the bathroom.

Seemingly disgusted, she looked up at me and said, "You were asleep already?"

I groaned as I shuffled across the floor leading to the bathroom. To my further surprise, everyone else was still up too. I could hear Mom and Devon's obnoxiously loud conversation about today's events, and my brothers were still playing that damn video game. I felt like the oldest one in the house for falling asleep earlier than everyone else, but then again, I always felt like the whole weight of the world was on my shoulders. That's how my depression made me feel. Or maybe I actually *did* have the weight of the world on my shoulders from being a full-time student and "mom" and a part-time chauffer, cook, nurse, and mediator. How could one juggle so much at one time? Receiving early life lessons on being a mom was not meant for everyone, especially those who didn't ask for it.

I made haste going to the bathroom in fear that being awake too long might keep me up the rest of the night. My body had this weird reaction that if it was awake for too long (including bathroom trips) in the middle of the night, it wouldn't allow me to go back to sleep. It was one of my many flaws, which was why I made it a point to keep my eyes closed during these middle-of-the-night trips so my body would feel like it was still asleep even if I wasn't.

I sleepily shuffled my way back into my sister's brightly lit room. She hadn't moved from her spot since I last saw her over a minute ago. Raven was still cracking up laughing at some random show that was being played on the Disney Channel, and for a moment, her little laughs brought me joy.

I opened the door to the attic—my door, the door that divided my room from my sister's—and stepped onto the first step, feeling the cracks in the floor give way to my foot. This place was old. With every step I took up to my room, I thought, *One day these damn stairs are just going to give way, and I'll fall right through to the first floor of the house. With my luck, I'll keep falling and land right-side up in the basement with everything crashing down on top of me.*

I arrived safely in my room with my eyes still closed and headed to my bed, even though my room was completely draped in darkness at that point. I felt my way around my bed and landed right back on the spot I'd left. *Hmm, still slightly warm from my body*, I thought. The comfort of falling back onto the warm spot soothed my soul.

I didn't know how long I'd lain there, but it was long enough for me to realize that I was now forcing myself to go back to sleep (deep sigh). This was why I hated going to the bathroom once I'd fallen into a deep sleep—that, and I hated being on the third floor. My warm spot now became overly warm, and I was forced to shift onto a less-warm spot to find comfort. With each shift, I became more and more alert to the fact that I was still awake. I could hear everything around me, and I didn't like it. My ability to hear everyone awake in this house was starting to irritate me because I felt like I shouldn't have been the only one fighting for sleep.

And worse, it wasn't even midnight yet, and I was begging my body to please go back to sleep.

All I could think about was the fact that I had school tomorrow, and the pressure of not knowing what was going to happen kept my mind active and uneasy. I didn't want to think about tomorrow or what I might have to do, but that was all I could do. *Did I have to take food out of the freezer before school to cook? Did I have to take one of my siblings somewhere after school for their enjoyment? Was Mom going to be home when I got home from school? Or was she planning on being gone all day?*

All these thoughts tumbled into in my mind at once, and I hated it. I shouldn't have been thinking about those things, but I had no way of shutting off my mind because I was sure to face all those scenarios sometime that week, whether it was tomorrow or the next day. My mind kept going, and I was still lying there with my eyes closed in the dark, forcing myself to go to sleep. It was getting to the point where I was ready to say, "Screw it," and turn the TV back on and just watch whatever was on until I felt the need to fall back to sleep.

Instead, I rolled over once more and tried to shift my mind to something a little less motherly. I could see my future, or at least the future I wanted in my head, and it was beautiful. My husband, who was a man I would probably never meet and only existed in my head, was gorgeous—too gorgeous to be with me. He was driving what I assumed was a car from that year, making me feel superior because I owned something so nice and new for once. We were happy and smiling at each other. I didn't know where we were going, but it didn't matter because we were happy.

This thought oddly put my mind at ease, and I could feel my body sink down into the mattress as I curled up into fetal position. I must have been really tensed up to physically feel my body sink down into the mattress. *How screwed up am I to make up such a thought just to put my mind at ease?*

At some point in the night, I must have rolled over onto my stomach because now I really had to pee again. I thought, *I was just in the bathroom, and I didn't drink anything. I haven't had anything to drink for hours now, so why does my bladder feel like I just had three bottles of water?*

I rolled back over onto my side, ignoring the fact that my bladder was about to burst. I hoped that if I ignored it long enough, I could go back to sleep and use the bathroom when it was time to get up.

But I couldn't ignore it, and it was still extremely dark outside. I had no idea what time it was or how long I'd actually been asleep, but it didn't feel like it had been for long. With my eyes still closed, I reached over to tap on my phone to bring it life. I cautiously opened one eye in fear that the screen would be too bright for my exhausted eyes. I looked in disgust and screamed at my inner self. It was only 3:30 a.m. I still had hours left of sleep before I had to get up for school.

"What the hell?" I said to myself. "It's not even close to time for me to get up for school, and yet I feel like I've slept for hours when it's only been about five."

I closed my eyes in hopes that I would fall into a deep sleep. I hoped my body would ignore the fact that I had to go to the bathroom so I could make it through the rest of the night without having to get up and take the walk of shame down the flight of stairs.

But now that my mind knew I had to go to the bathroom, that was all my body was physically letting me feel—a full-ass bladder. I rolled over in exhaustion and expressed disgust by throwing my duvet onto the other side of my bed. I moaned that I was doing this again five hours later when all I wanted was to go to sleep and stay asleep—at least for a few more hours.

I dragged my body from the comfort of yet another warm spot, like a zombie from a horror film. Eyes still closed, I used my feet to feel around for my slippers. *Why is the opening for my feet turned in the opposite direction?* I sighed deeply at the thought of this, scolding my inner self once more for being so stupid with positioning my slippers after my last bathroom trip.

I felt like an old, decrepit hermit crab slowly coming out of its shell. Sliding my feet into my slippers, I slowly rose and shuffled across the carpeted floor while feeling nothing but pure exhaustion. I tried to keep my eyes closed to prevent my body from feeling like it was time to wake up, but it wasn't that easy this time because I already felt like I'd slept long enough. *Ugh!* My body was failing me, making me feel a lot older than I actually was.

As I headed down the twelve steps to my sister's room, I could still hear the TV on. I guessed at this point that she and Raven were now asleep. But to my surprise, when I opened the door, they were both still very wide awake. Raven was still caught up in the Disney Channel, and my sister was now giving her full, undivided attention to whatever was on her phone.

I rolled my eyes in disgust at the sight of them still wide awake and not even looking the slightest bit tired. For God's sake, it was 3:00 a.m. Why were they still awake?

I ignored the side eye my sister gave me as I shuffled toward the door of her room. Before I could even step out, I heard the loud crashing of virtual bombs being thrown in my brothers' room.

At this point, I didn't even have the strength to roll my eyes anymore at the thought of my brothers still being awake—nor my sister. My eyes were now fully open, appreciating the darkness throughout the house. Judging by the light escaping from the bottom of their door, I assumed Mom and Devon were in their room. It was interesting how when it was just my brother and me, we had to be home before the streetlights came on. However, after the last two she seemed not to care as much, as long as we all made it to school on time without her having to drive us.

I headed to the bathroom and grabbed a piece of toilet paper to wipe the sleep from my eyes. I'd officially had my eyes open for too long, and now they were burning, and tears were running down my cheeks. That was another reason I preferred to keep my eyes closed while I was roaming around the house in the middle of the night. I didn't know why my eyes were irritated, but I hoped I wasn't the only one who experienced this. I tossed the piece of toilet paper into the toilet and took my seat. The relief of my bladder was a bit loud—louder than I'd expected.

I was now fully awake, and it was only 3:30 a.m. I had exactly four hours of sleep left, and the thought of not being able to complete those last hours of sleep haunted me. I went through this every night, and I didn't know why my body deceived me like this. I figured I should probably express this to my doctor the next time I saw her, but I rarely got sick or felt the need to see my own doctor because who the hell has the time to feel sick?

I sat there on the toilet hearing curse words flying out of the mouths of my brothers. I slouched over with my fist under my chin and wondered where they'd learned such words (and over a game at that). I gave myself the minute I needed to regain my focus and strength to head back upstairs to most likely lie there in the dark. Because now I wasn't the slightest bit tired, and the thought of not being able to fall back asleep was pissing me off.

I headed back into my sister's room where I was surprised to see that Raven was now tucked away under my sister's breast fast asleep. *Boy, how long was I in that bathroom?*

My sister briefly looked up from her phone, and then she quickly turned her gaze back to it. I supposed I didn't interest her as much. I put a little more pep in my step to make it up the twelve stairs to my room, now that I was fully awake.

Since I was now feeling myself, I walked a bit faster up the stairs than usual. I walked with such speed in the dark that I thought I'd try doing it the way my brothers did it and skip every other step to make it up there faster. Needless to say, I was not my brothers, and I didn't have the leg strength to skip every other step in the dark, nor should I have been skipping every other step to begin with.

I almost made it back into my room safely. A little bump on the shin never hurt anyone. I hobbled back to my bed, winced from the pain of hitting my shin on the hard end of a step, and shamed myself for trying to be like my brothers. I was familiar with walking around my room with my eyes closed, but I also knew it all too well with them open.

I slipped back into my bed, disappointed that I was gone long enough for my warm body imprint to be a thing of the past. I mentally went back to the make-believe time I had with my made-up husband to find enough inner peace to fall back to sleep for four more hours, and what do you know? It worked. I blissfully drifted away and awoke a few hours later facing the window to see that daylight had graced me with its presence. I sighed at the feeling of sleeping way longer than I actually did and thought to myself, *Another day.*

Chapter 9
Senior Year

With the vision of graduating, going to the best Ivy League universities, and being all that we could be, high school was almost a thing of the past. For me, it meant being able to finally get out of my mother's house and into my own without the responsibility of having to play mother hen. Senior year, for most, meant being able to leave school after second, third, or fourth period and doing whatever they wanted. For me, now that I had my driver's license, it meant being able to leave school and go right to work by picking up the slack of whatever my mother said she didn't have time to do. I know I shouldn't complain because it meant I was trusted to have such responsibility. However, for me, it only meant, *Now that you're older, you can fully take over my life as a mother. Do everything but my boyfriend.*

I started driving my mom's Grand Marquis when I was 14 years old, running her errands—even after dark. She taught me to drive, and when I turned 16, I got my driver's license. Mom had me running everywhere she didn't want to be when it came to my younger siblings. It was "do this; do that; go here; pick this up, and don't forget to grab that on your way home." It wasn't like I was being invited out to cool parties by kids in school. It wasn't like I had friends to hang out with either, but if I did, I was sure my mother would make me take at least one of my siblings with me.

I had no life, no friends, and no future while I was still at home. The one time I tried to do something for myself, it quickly backfired into oblivion.

It seemed like my mother did anything and everything to try and keep me from having a life of my own. I remember one time, my cousin Jessica and I had gone to the mall just to hang out, free of responsibility and siblings. We walked into a shoe store and were just browsing, not sure that either of us were actually going to buy anything, but I spotted some cute black pumps with silky lace going down the side. I was excited that they had a pair in my size, since I was born with big feet. I couldn't wait to take them home and show my mother how cute they were. I don't know why, but the kid in me came out over a pair of shoes. The moment I showed them to my mom, the feeling that I had impressed her with the shoes was lost. She took one look at them and then back at me, and with a completely straight face, she said, "Do I need to go out and buy you some condoms to go with those shoes?"

I felt completely stupid for ever being excited to show her what I'd bought. I hadn't even lost my virginity yet, and she was questioning my promiscuity based on a pair of shoes.

I said, "Mom, they're just shoes."

She repeated her statement again, this time with a little more pitch in her voice, as if she were daring me to say it again.

The next day, I asked my cousin to come back with me to the mall so I could return the shoes. I didn't need them anyway. Where was I ever going to wear them? It wasn't like I had friends to go out with. I'd never returned anything because I rarely bought things for myself. So, when I walked into the shoe store and saw the same woman who had sold them to me the day before, I panicked. I quickly looked at my cousin and asked her what I should say as a believable reason for returning the shoes. My cousin was always quick on her feet with replies such as this one, and she told me to lie and tell her that I'd changed my mind about them.

As I approached the lady, butterflies settled into my stomach, making me feel sick for what I was about to do. I was so nervous that I damn near shoved the bag back into her hands. I felt like she could see right through me, and knew I was about to lie.

She took the box out of the bag and asked if I had the receipt. I nervously told her everything was inside the bag. She went for the receipt first and looked it over like she was scanning it for something wrong. Then she took the shoes out of the box one by one and looked at the backs of them. I grabbed my stomach, trying to keep myself from throwing up, because I'd put the shoes on to model for my unpleased mother. When the lady turned the left one over, I noticed a scuff mark on the back of it, and I went into full panic mode because I noticed a sign that said worn shoes couldn't be returned to the store. She looked at the shoe and rubbed her thumb across it and then glanced back up at me like she knew. I looked over at my cousin with wide eyes and just knew it was over.

The lady placed both shoes back into the box, and I prepared for her to hand them back to me and say, "No, thank you," but she didn't. She set them aside, processed my return, gave me my full refund, and told me to have a nice day with a reserved smile that I was sure she gave all customers who tried to pull one over on her.

My cousin and I quickly left the store without looking back, like we had just stolen something and were in a hurry to get away. I always wondered why the lady gave me my money back when the evidence of them being worn was there. Maybe she didn't feel like arguing with me, or maybe she just took pity on two school-aged girls and thought we needed the money. Either way, leave it to my mother to kill my joy. She had a habit of doing that. No matter what I did, I could never impress her or live up to her standards. I don't know if she did it to make herself feel better, or if she just enjoyed crushing my spirit so I wouldn't be happy, since she wasn't happy.

I had a habit of letting the bad things weigh heavily on my mind for long periods of time, and the same went for grudges. I could hold a grudge like none other. Everyone always says it's good to forgive and forget or forgive, but not forget. Either way, the fact that I felt guilty for so long after taking back those shoes because of my mother's perception of them, when they were just shoes, brought out the worst in me most days.

Now, don't get me wrong. This wasn't just about shoes bringing out the worst in me. It was about everything that my mother had ever put me through over the years, and it had finally come to this. There was more bad than good, like being told by my mother that she wished she'd never given birth to me. Her absence due to partying and meeting strange men showed that they were more important than raising her two young kids. I'd seen her ignore what she'd turned me into, and I struggled with my inability to have a conversation with her about my experience when I was younger. And now this…

Those damn shoes that I really liked and wanted were now back on the shelf at the shoe department for ten dollars less than what I first purchased them for. I don't know what pissed me off more—the fact that those shoes were now on clearance for $39.99 and I'd paid more for them, or the fact that they were only on sale because I stupidly let my mother's antics get to me, forcing me to return them. I didn't know how then, but now I know how to get rid of a scuff mark on the back of a shoe before returning it, not that it matters.

Eventually, those shoes became a thing of the past, not that they still weren't weighing heavily on my mind. But my mother found other distractions to keep me busy, like who I was going to invite to my graduation since the school only allowed five tickets per child. So, choosing who'd be allowed to come to my graduation was like choosing who could come to my wedding. Either way, somebody's feelings were going to be hurt. Luckily, I didn't have a very big pool to choose from, and unfortunately, that pool became smaller and smaller.

Everyone I invited to go to my graduation had respectfully declined because either their grandchild or someone they knew was graduating that same day. My own grandparents couldn't even go, so in the end, the one person who despised me the most and took pleasure in making my life feel less than was going to be a one-woman cheering squad. But to make matters worse, senior year was halfway over, and I still hadn't experienced any of my "firsts" yet.

I didn't go to prom, I didn't get asked to prom, and I spent all of ten minutes at homecoming because my date, who was Marty at the time, had to go home. I still hadn't had my first boyfriend, I'd never been kissed, I was still a virgin, and I still hadn't been invited to any cool high school parties. But at this point, none of that seemed to matter. I figured there was a reason why I hadn't lost my virginity yet: All of the boys in school were either intimidated by me or only saw me as that one cool friend they could come to for their girlfriend problems.

So, in the end, I said, "Screw it. Just focus on finishing school and getting good grades so you can get the hell out of here and out of Martinsburg for good. My time will come when I'm ready for a boyfriend, whenever that is."

But to be honest, I wasn't exactly the swan in *Swan Lake*. I was more like the ugly duckling who never outgrew it. The only guys who found me attractive were the ones who were way too old for me and only wanted sex. But since I was so determined to keep my virginity until marriage, I didn't let any of that phase me.

That said, if we were talking about the old Tozaneé, who wanted nothing more than love and affection, the old guys back then might have won. At one point in my life, I thought all I needed to be happy was a man, or at least someone to tell me that I was pretty. Between my fluctuating weight, my big nose, and my high testosterone levels that kept hair on my face, under my chin, and on my chest, guys had multiple reasons not to be with me—no matter how hard I tried to look normal to the naked eye.

As the seasons changed, so did my many moods. But the fall, the fall is what changed my mood completely.

I was not only born in the fall, but the atmosphere itself was also what I loved the most. I loved watching the ever-changing leaves cover the ground in bright oranges and reds with a touch of green and the feel of the cool fall wind hitting my bare skin. That was what I looked forward to the most. The air just felt cleaner in the fall. It made me feel more alive and eager to go outside with just one look and sensation from the air.

Nevertheless, I hated birthdays—mine in particular. Especially, since I was stripped of having birthday parties at the age of thirteen. So, when my birthday rolled around in the fall of that year, it was no surprise that turning eighteen just felt like any other birthday. It was a normal day, and I went to school that morning like I did every morning. Mom was nowhere in sight, so I didn't get a "happy birthday" on my way out the door. Instead, I walked to school alone with both relief and sadness, at the same time, because Marty had either gotten a head start, or he'd gotten a ride to school, which happened often towards the end of the schoolyear.

No one in school knew who I was because I didn't stick out like a sore thumb or make a big impression. So, when I finally arrived at school, I saw everyone standing outside in big crowds like they usually did before the first bell rang for everyone to go inside. I found the crowd of usual girls my cousin, Jessica, was standing in and decided to join them. Hey, I had nothing else better to do at the time, and everyone was slowly walking inside at the sound of the first bell, so why not?

Before I could join them, someone gestured in my direction, and they all simultaneously turned around and looked right at me, giving me that uneasy feeling. I hated being the center of attention. It made me feel self-conscious. I often got the worst cramps in my abdomen or what some might call "butterflies," and my heart would start to race.

A few feet away from joining the giggling girls, my cousin sounded off by saying, "Eyyyyy." The sound soon made its way around the circle of girls, gradually growing louder and louder, drawing more attention in my direction.

"HAPPY BIRTHDAY, Cuz!" Jessica yelled out, starting a wave of "Happy Birthday, Tozaneé greetings from the other girls, who only knew of me through her, which made it seem a little odd coming from them. They didn't usually speak to me or hang out with me on the regular like they did with my cousin, but who doesn't like saying "happy birthday" to a stranger on their birthday?

I tried hard not to let the excitement of being acknowledged for a split second get to me, but I couldn't shake the stupid grin off my face. Sadly, because I knew this would be the only time I would get such acknowledgment from anyone outside of my family, after being told "happy birthday" by numerous passersby who had overheard the commotion, we headed inside, and we all went in opposite directions to homeroom.

Homeroom was the spot to chill before first period. It was where we heard the daily announcements, the menu for lunch, and the replays on last night's game (mostly football related). But Homeroom was also where all the cool kids, who mainly sat in the back, planned their next trip or house party because someone's parents were either going to be out of town for that week or their parents said they could have a small get-together, which would turn into every cool person being invited from every school in our district.

I sat in the back up against a wall where I could listen to all the excitement of their party planning, hoping that one day one of them would eventually look in my direction and invite me. *Wishful thinking, girl!* I'd been invisible my whole life and all four years of high school. Why would they notice me now? No matter how much I liked being unnoticeable, I also hated being unnoticeable. I think it came from when I was kid, and my mom would often say that she wanted to hear me but not see me.

Now that I'm older, most days I'm both; I can't be seen or heard, which I find weird when I think about it because I was a very quiet kid too. Most days, I was so quiet that people thought something was wrong with me because I didn't want to speak or interact with other kids my age. But that's just the nature of it for me, I guess. I learned a lot by being quiet and unseen, even some things that I probably shouldn't have heard from my mom and her friends.

But here I was, sitting in the back of homeroom, eager to be seen just to take away one high school experience. If nothing else, why not let it be a party?

I was stuck in my own little world of being an outsider amongst the cool kids when the bell rang, signaling that it was time for first period. I shook away the thought of ever being one of them and walked the long hallway to first period, which was math—and it sucked. I hated math and everything about it. After leaving my first period class, I pulled out my phone to check the time to see how much longer I had before the bell rang. Upon checking for the time, I noticed that I had an unopened message.

Hmm, I said to myself because no one ever texted me. I didn't even know why I had a phone half the time.

It was a message from my mom, wishing me a happy birthday and a great day. Before replying, I noticed other missed messages in my phone. They were from more family members, wishing me the same. The love made the corners of my cheeks rise. I was going through all of my messages when the bell finally rang for second period. Boy, that took longer than I'd expected.

I walked halfway down the hall to my next class. The hallways quickly filled with eager students in pursuit of their next period. Some were looking for their friends before continuing on.

Second period was my next-to-last period before I was done for the day, so when it came time for second period, I was ready to leave school. But I never really wanted to go home because there was nothing there for me, so I avoided going home at all costs. I knew if I didn't go home, there'd be no one to take care of the kids because asking Mom if she was home or not was never an option, and I knew Devon wasn't going to watch my siblings because he saw them as "not my problem."

There was something about being home without my mother that scared me. I always felt uneasy when she wasn't around or when I didn't hear her voice. I know having my siblings there should have helped to ease some of my fear, but it didn't because they were stuck in their own little worlds of video games or constantly straightening their hair and trying on every shade of makeup. I tried to reassure myself by thinking that I was giving myself high anxiety about being home without the presence of my mother, and time and time again, I'd proven myself right.

It simply did not feel right, not knowing where my mother was or when she'd return. The uneasiness I felt was heightened around a bunch of men and didn't do well for my anxiety either. I didn't know what I was going to see when I walked through that door. It could have been an empty living room, Devon and all of his friends playing loud music and yelling over the music to communicate, Mom doing someone's hair, or Mom cooking in the kitchen. I didn't know what I was going to get most days. It was like a never-ending adventure that I was never really ready for; shit just happened.

By the end of second period, the need to go home was dire. I didn't have a job yet since today was my eighteenth birthday, and although Mom let me drive her car, I had nowhere to go after school except home. I mean, I could've gotten something to eat for lunch since I was no longer at school long enough to actually eat lunch, but there were only so many places to choose from, and it wasn't like I had a taste for anything special.

Third period came and went just like that because my anxiety made it fly by, so by the time the bell rang, most kids headed towards the cafeteria for the start of lunch, and others, like me, headed in another direction to leave. I walked out of the front door, which overlooked the main street heading into the town of Martinsburg, and I stood on the curb and watched all the other kids, who drove to school that morning, exchange pleasantries with their friends before jumping into their cars and pulling off. I looked in the direction of home and let out a deep sigh because once again, the thought of going home was very depressing, and no one should feel like they can't or shouldn't go home.

I walked down the driveway leading away from the school's campus, and I turned around to see how far I'd gotten from the building. Sadly, I think I'd only made it one hundred feet. I looked into the distance and noticed that the trees were moving as the wind was blowing, but I didn't feel a thing. It was the perfect fall morning. It was still early in the day (no more than 10:30 a.m.), and it felt blissful as I enjoyed my short stroll home.

I usually took about twenty to twenty-five minutes to get from school to home and vice versa, but today… Today, I thought I'd make that trip a little bit longer than usual. I took the time to appreciate the beautiful fall weather, kicking the leaves that were cascading across the ground, listening to the crunch of them under my feet. God, I loved fall and everything about it. If it were any other season, like summer or winter, my walk home from school would've been a lot more brisk, but today I wanted to take in and feel all that fall had to offer.

My venture towards home was getting closer and closer, but the fall weather made me not care. Right then in that moment, I felt good, and all my worries faded away into the cool breeze. The walk home put an unexpected smile on my face. I wondered why I was smiling, but I didn't care to know. People driving past me probably thought I was insane or were hoping that I was looking at something to put that smile on my face and not just smiling for no reason. But who cares? I was doing something I didn't normally do. I was smiling. I was walking home when I really didn't want to, and I was smiling.

I turned the corner that was near the cemetery and walked slower, giving myself time to read the names on the tomb stones. I hated walking past cemeteries because they creeped me out, but this time, I found myself reading the names of those who had once lived. Some of the names made me laugh because I wondered how they came up with such names. Others gave me chills because they were the last names of other family members, and they made me think.

As I walked past the cemetery, I could see the courthouse on the right. Next to that was the county sheriff's department on the left. Funny how they said the city was on a budget every year to buy fireworks for the Fourth of July, but they could find money to build a brand-new building for the sheriff's department along with new cars. Even today, it makes me wonder where my personal property taxes are really going, especially since every time I pay them, I have to make the check or money order out to the sheriff's department.

Once the courthouse and sheriff's department were in my sights, I knew that my home was just a straight shot downhill from there. I stopped and looked back, wondering if I should retrace my steps to make my walk home even longer. I looked uphill and could see my mom's car was there, which relieved some of my anxiety and pressure to go home. So, I decided to carry on with my journey and caught myself wondering why she was home. I wondered if she was just home for right now, or if she would be leaving later on in the day.

As I headed downhill towards home, the wind hit me twice as hard, not because the wind was blowing harder, but because I was going down a steep hill pretty fast. As I approached the end of the hill, I felt like I'd just ran a mini race. I was breathing a little bit harder, and my calf muscles and feet felt like I'd just done some lifting. I paused at the corner by the stop sign to check for oncoming cars and get a much-needed breather.

Once I'd regained my breath and I knew for certain that there were no cars coming, I proceeded with caution. Walking down the hill was a breeze, literally, but walking back up to get home was another story. If I thought my calf muscles and feet were feeling uncomfortable now, I was really in for a treat walking back up. Not only did I hate living on the very top floor of my home, but this hill was also out to get me. It just constantly reminded me every day that I needed to lose weight.

I defeated the hill once again, but now I was super out of breath and silently cursing at it. I walked up the six steps leading to the front door of my house and thought about how seriously out of shape I was because that wasn't even the end of it, and I was already tired. When I stuck the key in the door and turned, I noticed that the door wasn't even locked because I didn't get that clicking sound you get when you turn the key.

I opened the door, and my mom looked straight up and said loudly, "The door wasn't locked."

I didn't say a word. I just shut the door behind me and walked through the living room. I noticed that the TV was on some cartoon channel, but no one was watching it. I also saw the reason why Mom was still there and not someplace else. She had a woman in the chair, and she was doing her hair. On my right, Devon was also cutting someone's hair in his chair. I tried to walk past Mom like a turtle refusing to come out of its shell to keep from being noticed.

But I didn't get too far when Mom yelled, "Happy birthday!"

The woman in her chair looked up from her phone while furiously chewing her gum and kindly told me the same thing.

I nervously looked away, mumbled a "thank you" under my breath, and veered off towards the steps.

I got about halfway up the stairs when I heard Mom yell, "How was school?"

I paused and yelled, "It was fine."

"Did anyone do anything special for you since it was your birthday?" she asked.

"No," I said, as I turned to head upstairs.

"Well, why not?"

I sadly said, "Because, I'm not popular," while trying to mask the pain in my voice.

"You don't have to be popular for kids at school to do things for you on your birthday."

I tried hard to end this awkward and sad conversation by saying, "I don't know, Mom."

As I walked the rest of the way up the stairs, I could hear Mom mumbling to her client that it was sad how kids don't do spontaneous things like that anymore, and when she was in school on her birthday, her girlfriends did cool things for her all the time. Overhearing that reminded me of how sad of a person I was to not have those types of cool friends in my life, and I knew exactly what she was talking about.

I saw kids celebrated by their friends at school all the time on their birthdays. You could usually tell when it was someone's birthday at school because they were usually walking down the hallway with a bouquet of balloons in one hand and carrying a cake with the other. Some went all out and wore a tiara and a sash around their bodies, displaying the words *Birthday Princess* or *Birthday Girl*. I guess I just wasn't lucky enough to have friends like that. Olivia may have done something, but she was at a different school.

I opened the door that divided my room from my sister's and closed it behind me, encasing me in pure, total darkness. I thought, *This is where I belong—in the dark. Out of sight, out of mind.*

My depression kicked in, and I was enveloped in nothing but pure, total sorrow. I was sad that my mother voiced her disappointment in how kids were nowadays and my knowing that it wasn't the kids—it was me. People just didn't like me. My mom had a daughter who was boring and anti-social, a daughter who couldn't find friends to hang out with after school instead of coming home.

Here I was, eighteen and finally an adult, and I was depressed now more than ever, and it was my birthday. I shouldn't have been depressed on my birthday, but I was alone in my room. I wondered why I wasn't liked, what I was doing wrong, and what people saw when they looked at me to automatically decide that I wasn't worth befriending. I was a good person. I was literally the kind of person who would give someone my last dollar, but no one knew it—or seemed to care.

I'd let people use me in the past for rides because they knew that I drove, and they'd literally hop out and not give me gas money. But I never said anything about it because I was just that kind of person. So what was I doing wrong to be sitting in my room by myself on my eighteen birthday, a birthday that every girl dreamed of celebrating because it was the first step into adulthood? Happy freaking birthday to me!

I smelled food, and it smelled amazing. I rolled over onto my stomach. I must have fallen asleep at some point while basking in my own state of depression. But now that my body was awake, minus my eyes being open, I felt a strong urge to go and pee, and when I say *strong*, I mean *strong*.

I jumped out of bed with great speed and quickly stumbled my way into my slippers, tripping over one during this quest. My second slipper was finally on, and I ran towards the curtain covering the opening of my bedroom door.

I flipped the switch that brought the overhead lights bursting to life, making me wince from the brightness above after falling asleep. I trailed down the stairs so quickly that I felt as if I were about to fall over. I swung open the door that lent privacy between me and my sister's room, only to startle both my sister and Raven with my less-than-elegant entrance. My sister was sitting in her usual spot, at her mirror, while straightening her hair again for the millionth time, and Raven was, of course, watching our favorite show, *Phineas and Ferb,* on the Disney Channel.

I swung open my sister's bedroom door as if someone were chasing me out of the room, and I stumbled around the hallway entrance like I'd just had too much to drink the previous night. Grateful that it wasn't occupied for once, I flew into the bathroom and slammed the door behind me while trying to pull down my pants at the same time.

What the hell did I drink? I asked myself, feeling as if my bladder was about to burst any minute. I was going for the toilet when I missed the landing and slid off the edge of the seat. I cursed myself for being so clumsy at a time like this.

My body didn't even give me a split second to adjust my composure before releasing the pressure, and I found myself exclaiming "ahhh" out loud. This was my sign of relief from my overly full bladder, which still had me puzzled because I couldn't remember drinking anything at all. But while I was sitting there, the wonderful smell of food filled the air and momentarily distracted me from the fact that I was still peeing.

I didn't know who the hell was cooking downstairs, but it smelled mouth-watering. Judging by the aroma, I was convinced that it was probably tacos, but at that point, it could've been anything. I'd also forgotten the fact that it was my birthday, and whatever was being made downstairs probably had nothing to do with it. Mom used to make us whatever we wanted for our birthdays, but she never asked me what I wanted this morning or when I came home, so it was probably just something random and easy for her to make for the whole house.

I sat there trying to replay what I possibly could have had to drink that day. It was getting to the point where I was becoming annoyed because it was all I could focus on. My mind would do that to me a lot, making me feel as if I had a form of ADHD or ADD.

I had a problem with shutting my mind off, but I think that's all women, period. Once we have something on our minds, we find ourselves endlessly focusing on that same thought for long periods of time.

I sat there for so long that my legs felt as if they were about to fall asleep, which was a sign that I needed to get up before they made it even harder for me to walk. I leaned forward to turn on the faucet so the water would warm before I got up to wash my hands. I slowly got up, feeling as if sitting there had somehow aged me at least twenty years.

The water was piping hot, judging from the abundance of steam coming from it. I looked at the frail, broken woman in the mirror. *That's right. I'm officially a woman as of today!* The thought came across like a freight train, giving me a split second to appreciate that I had made it eighteen years on Earth. My face looked like I'd slept all day and judging by the lines going across my right cheek, I'd slept on something pretty hard. My hair looked like I'd just been in a fight because one side was still in a ponytail, and the other was loose and messy. The sleep in and around my eyes portrayed the look and feel that I'd slept all day and all night when it had just been a few hours…if that.

I grabbed my washcloth from the shower behind me and ran it under the scalding water, as I appreciated the sting and relaxation at the same time. I wiped my face from bottom to top, starting at the base of my neck and wiping my way up to my eyes while gently rubbing the sleep from them. I rinsed the rag and went back for a second gentle rub around my eyes, making sure to get all the sleep from them.

Lastly, I dabbed the grease from my forehead, making me look like a new woman all over again. I didn't look like I'd been asleep at all today, so I couldn't allow the look of being asleep now. I folded the rag to dry, placed it back in the shower, and ran my hands under the hot water again, giving me one last wonderful sensation before turning the faucet off. I reached for the door, but I'd forgotten that I'd slammed it closed earlier in my rush to the toilet, so now the top part of the door was stuck in the door frame, making me pull harder and throwing me back a little once it opened.

The smell of food was stronger in the air now, and I wondered if I should go downstairs to see what was being made. I tried to walk downstairs without making a noise so I wouldn't draw attention to myself, but the old-ass stairs creaked at every step, making me hate myself for really being overweight. I made it down the last stairs, and the first thing I saw was Devon sitting in his barber chair, brushing his own hair and staring in the mirror at himself. I walked by thinking, *Conceited much, are we?*

I even found myself holding my breath, as I walked past him in hopes that he didn't strike up the nerve to talk to me because he always said something smart or sarcastic. But trying hard to be invisible failed. He spotted me stepping down the last stair and waited until I was walking in the kitchen to say, "Hi, Toza," in his most sarcastic, annoying voice.

I pretended like I didn't hear him and kept it moving towards the kitchen. Mom looked up from the stove and noticed me standing in the doorway. She looked at me oddly and said, "Were you asleep?"

"Yes," I said in an almost scratchy voice.

She replied, "Huh! You don't look like you were asleep."

I almost cursed myself for wiping all signs of my being asleep away in the bathroom. I slowly crept over to the stove like a dog with its tail between its legs and looked to see that she was frying ground beef in a skillet. I hoped the ground beef was for tacos, but before I made that assumption, I looked around the kitchen to see if I could make out the fixings to go with it.

It looked like my assumptions were correct. Tacos for dinner it was. I couldn't tell if she was making them for me since it was my birthday and tacos were one of my favorite foods, or if she was just doing it because it could easily feed a family of eight.

I looked around the kitchen like a wandering child, hoping the next thing I'd see was a cake, but then a part of me wondered if I was too old for a birthday cake. I didn't see one on the table behind Mom, but as I was walking into the kitchen, she told me not to walk too hard or I'd make the cake in the oven fall.

I felt like a tender-aged schoolgirl, getting one of her favorite dinners and a homemade cake for her birthday. I turned on my heels to safely leave the kitchen and focused all my attention on making it back upstairs without Devon making another cocky remark. He didn't say anything, but his eyes met mine and, in an attempt to ignore him, I picked up the pace to make it back upstairs. As I was walking back up the stairs, I could hear his creepy, old, perverted laugh, like he'd just defeated me in a staring contest. What the hell was he always laughing about? He always laughed for no reason. I was starting to think either his past drug use was catching up to him, or he was using again, because no one laughs at themselves unless they're mentally incompetent.

Cursing myself for being slightly out of breath, I made it all the way up the stairs and opened the door to my sister's room. I found her still sitting in the same spot doing her hair and Raven sitting at full attention, staring at the TV.

Feeling fully awake now, I opened the door that divided our rooms and headed up another flight of stairs. I was walking up the stairs with a little pep in my step because I was pleased about the dinner that I was getting, along with the cake that Mom was baking in the oven. I remembered the last time she made me a birthday cake was on my thirteenth birthday. How dry that cake was that even her friends, whom she invited, refused to eat it. I'd seen both the professional and personal cakes she'd made over the years since then, so I hoped mine looked and tasted as good as the cakes she'd made for her clients.

I was back in the comfort and safety of my room. I looked around for the remote now that I was fully awake, expecting to also watch some *Phineas and Ferb*, but as soon as I turned on the TV and went straight to the Disney Channel, I was disappointed to see that it had gone off and something else was on. In my disappointment, I found myself searching for something else. The Cooking Channel… You could never go wrong with the Cooking Channel, and *Diners, Drive-Ins and Dives* was on.

I put the remote down and curled up into fetal position, placing my left hand between my thighs for comfort and my right hand under my pillow to support my head. I was lost in the excitement of what was on TV when the thought of checking my phone crossed my mind. I rolled my eyes at the thought of it because no one ever talked to me. Still, I reached for my phone anyway, and it instantly vibrated to life in my hand, letting me know that I had a missed message.

I hoped that was actually a missed text message from someone other than my mom, but from whom? I woke my phone up and saw the envelope icon on my screen. It was indeed a missed text. Wondering who would've messaged me, I unlocked my phone and hit the icon. It was from Jessica, asking what I was doing.

I was somewhat intrigued but not as excited as I would have been if it were from someone who didn't talk to me all the time like my cousin did.

I just woke up from a nap, and Mom

is making me a birthday dinner.

What's she making?

Tacos.

We were equally excited because, I swear, we were both born to eat tacos.

What kind?

Beef.

In my family, we do a variety when it comes to things like tacos. We have all the fixings to go with it, but nothing too fancy.

Jessica and I talked for a while with long pauses between responses from the both of us. Finally, my sister yelled that it was time for dinner. Before I could yell back, I heard the door being slammed shut. Moments later, I heard feet, like it was the great race to get downstairs for dinner.

I lay there for a moment to let the dust settle from the herd and continued to watch a little more TV before making my descent down the stairs for dinner. I knew that no matter how long I chose to stay upstairs before dinner, Mom wouldn't let the kids eat all the food before I had the chance to get to some, especially since it was my birthday, and I knew this dinner was for me. Other days, maybe, but not on my birthday.

I slowly made my way downstairs and was excited to see a skillet full of taco meat and a kitchen full of all the fixings waiting for me. In the living room, Mom and Devon were already halfway through their dinner, and in the kitchen, Raven turned to look at me with a face full of what I could only assume was salsa. She instantly giggled when she saw me, like she knew that I was staring at her salsa-covered face. I smiled to myself and thought this laughing thing between she and her father must've been hereditary.

I looked around at all the fixings laid out in the kitchen and wondered which route I should take as before—tacos or taco salad? Mom bought all the perfect fixings for either. I often decided to go in the taco salad direction, whether spicy or mild. I was so hungry that night, and looking at all the food made it harder to determine how big of a salad I actually wanted.

After properly preparing all of the ingredients, my taco salad looked so perfectly proportioned and well put together. I couldn't wait to sit down and eat it. I took my seat on the bench and dug in from the side, careful not to lift my fork too fast so that nothing flew out of the bowl. I wasn't even halfway through when I felt like I'd overdone it. *Maybe this bowl was a little too big.* My eyes, in this case, were definitely bigger than my belly.

I was in the middle of my bowl when all of the kids simultaneously got up and threw their plates away. *Without seconds!* My surprise was mainly due to the boys since they were the ones who could really eat now that they were all playing football. But it was no surprise that Raven finished everything on her plate and was now eyeballing my sister. I asked if she wanted some more, and in her tiny, shy voice, she said, "No." But she said it with a big grin, which confused me about if she was really still hungry or just waiting for my sister to finish.

My sister liked to eat slowly when she was on her phone, like she was savoring each bite of food, but what she really preferred was to eat slowly when she was just about done because she didn't want to get up and throw it away. She was eating so slowly that Raven was now trying to find things to distract herself. She swung her little legs back and forth, all while trying to make herself dizzy. She finally lost patience because she asked my sister when she was going to be done. My sister mumbled under her breath that she'd be done in a minute, but judging by her half-full plate and the deep conversation she was in, "in a minute" was a strong phrase to use.

I could tell Raven was quickly losing more patience because she kept looking in my direction, like she was asking for help. Her big puppy-dog eyes suggested she was either tired or upset for having to wait on someone she admired.

While my sister felt that she was too old to be friends with Raven, this little girl would disagree. She would do anything for my sister to keep her all to herself. I think it came from the lack of energy she was getting from her father, whom she would also do anything for. Sadly, I knew all too well how Raven felt.

After losing hope and energy, Raven finally got up from the table and walked over to the trash to throw away her plate. As she stomped her way out of the kitchen, now frustrated, she yelled back at my sister without looking in her direction that she was going to be upstairs waiting on her. I smiled because she was so damn feisty for a two-year-old, and she'd basically just said, "Forget it. I'm not waiting on you," to my sister, who still wasn't paying her any attention.

My sister and I sat there and finished our meals in complete silence. I wondered if she realized how she was treating Raven. A few minutes went by, and she got up from her spot at the table while mumbling under her breath that she was done. She walked over to the trash, tossed her plate inside, and tossed her fork into the sink.

It was just me who was left in the kitchen to enjoy the rest of my birthday meal in peace. I sat there in silence, looking at the wall in front of me, wondering what kind of cake Mom made me since it was now sitting on top of the oven to cool. There were four pans sitting on the stove. Unsure why there were there, I got up from my seat to sneak a peek, and I noticed they were all different colors: red, blue, green, and I assumed the last one was yellow, almost all the colors of the rainbow.

"Hmm," I said to myself, as I took my rightful seat back at the table to finish my dinner. I was just about done, and now I was really thinking I'd outdone myself this time and every time I ate something. *Portion control. I must learn portion control.*

I looked down at my impeding gut and tried to ignore the fact that I was fat and attempted to enjoy the last of my meal. Disappointed that the mini tortilla chips were now kind of soggy, I choked down the last few bites of my food. I got up from the table and tossed my plate into the trash. I placed my fork in the sink and walked past the rest of the food on the stove while wondering if I should put it away or leave it out just in case someone changed their mind and wanted seconds.

I headed towards the stairs when Mom called from the living room, "All done eating?"

"Yes," I told her and headed upstairs to rest my now-aching tummy.

The need to stay awake was crucial at this moment because eventually I was going to have birthday cake, and I didn't want to miss it, no matter how full I was. So, in a stronger effort to stay awake, I decided to take a shower.

It was still daytime outside, but who says you can't shower in the middle of the day? Plus, I wouldn't have to fight for the bathroom when everyone else in the house was ready for their baths. So, I grabbed my towel and headed down my stairs towards the bathroom.

My sister saw me on the way there with my towel, and as if she was disgusted, she said, "You're already getting a shower?"

"I'm in the bathroom already running the hot water," I replied without looking back.

Already feeling the weight of the world falling off my shoulders, I stripped off my clothes and let them hit the tops of my feet and the floor. I stepped into the back of the shower, letting the water hit me slowly from the front instead of all at once. The feel of the hot water felt amazing. It felt even more incredible because the air conditioner was on full blast, and the vent was over my head, which mixed the cool of the air with the heat of the shower.

It felt so good to have the bathroom all to myself and not have to rush to save water for someone else. The feel of the water made me feel powerful in that moment. Because I felt so free, I questioned whether this was the time to wash my hair or not. Doing that would mean I'd have to spend at least an hour in the shower, and I knew how my mother felt about that.

Instead, when I felt like I'd reached my limit on showering, I turned the majestic water off and reached for my towel. I loosely wrapped it around my damp body and looked down before stepping out. Grabbing my clothes off the floor, I drew them close to my body before heading for the bathroom door. Again, the damn thing was jammed shut, forcing me to pull harder and drawing my body back a few inches from the opening. The door burst open, echoing throughout the rest of the house and letting everyone know that someone was in the bathroom. I was immediately horrified and embarrassed by the sound on my way back through my sister's room and up the stairs.

I dried off the rest of my body and hung my towel to dry in its usual spot on my vanity mirror. I thought about whether I should get dressed right away. There were still some odd hours left till my birthday was over, and Mom hadn't yelled down for cake just yet, so I felt like I still had time.

Instead of getting dressed, I opted to sit on the edge of bed stark naked. I wasn't worried about anyone catching me since no one ever went up there to begin with.

I looked outside the window and noticed that the sun was just now starting to set on the horizon, giving it that calm, relaxing feel outside. There was a tree outside my window, and the leaves were barely hanging onto its branches while the base of the tree was surrounded by the leaves that had already fallen. I wished we could have fall weather all year round. There was just something about it that I admired more than any of the other seasons.

Not only is fall beautiful, but it also has a timeless look—all things fall.

Chapter 10
F.A.T.

After sitting naked on my bed for some time, I found myself feeling a little exposed and decided it was finally time to put on some clothes. I was literally in my own room, and I felt "exposed." What the hell was wrong with me? I was uncomfortable in any situation, but for me to feel uncomfortable about being naked in my own room (especially right after I was just sitting there comfortably for some time before the thought crossed my mind) was a bit strange.

I'm one weird individual, I thought. *It's no wonder I have no friends, but sadly, I can also feel my gut sitting on my lap, and that alone is unpleasant.*

I walked over to my sitting vanity mirror that never made it onto the back of my dresser and gazed upon the overweight woman I'd become. I squeezed here and there on my stomach. Being able to lift it and feel it slamming back down against my body was just sickening. I didn't understand how I'd become so big. But then the thought of a once-sickly looking child who was constantly made fun of for being Black and having a big nose crossed my mind.

That thought, combined with the fact that I had to become a mother hen at such a young age to all of my siblings just so my mother could continue living her life, didn't make my weight any better. I was in a house full of endless snacks and microwavable foods; plus, we were constantly going out to buffets. Add that to no exercise (aside from walking to school and back home) because the fear of going outside led me to stay inside and only made my weight worse, and it was even harder to take the weight off—especially when I was diagnosed with Type 2 Diabetes.

    I could only stand in front of the mirror for so long before I felt physically ill and started to tell myself that the mirror added ten pounds. But, then again, how long can you keep telling yourself this before it just becomes denial? I needed to stop telling myself this bullshit because it wasn't the mirror; it was me—*all me*. I was starting to really see the ugly side of myself and why I didn't have friends. Who would want to be friends with someone who looked like me?

    If I physically made myself violently ill just from the sight of my own body, I didn't want to imagine what others thought when they saw me. I quickly threw on a pair of shorts and an old t-shirt because I now actually did think I was going to throw up from looking at myself in the mirror. I headed towards the curtain when I stopped myself and tried to take a deep, cleansing breath to see if calming my nerves would distract my mind from running to the bathroom. I felt my heart rate slowing down, so I backtracked towards my bed and sat down on the edge to focus on the TV. Ironically, *Chopped* was still on. I wondered if it was a marathon or if they were just playing a lot of episodes for no reason.

    Watching the Cooking Channel helped momentarily, but when I looked away, my mouth started to water and my vision became clouded with falling tears. I couldn't believe the sight of my own body was doing this to me. I found myself rocking back and forth on the edge of the bed and humming a tune in an effort to keep myself from throwing up on my bedroom floor.

    Wow! No more thoughts of how disgusting I look from now on if this is what it's going to do to me, I thought.

The humming and rocking back and forth were working. I was starting to feel less sick to my stomach but not as fast as I would've liked. So, I kept humming and increased my rocking. At this point, I was squeezing my eyes shut because the tears kept falling. Eventually, the feeling was behind me like it never happened, and I felt the need to lie down on my bed to comfort myself. I pushed the thought of all things fat out of my mind and focused on the TV.

Great. I'm making myself sick about being fat while watching the Cooking Channel.

By the time I came to complete calmness, my room was almost completely cascaded in darkness. I was now wrapped up in my comforter in the fetal position with my left hand under my thigh and my right hand under my pillow. The buzz of my phone distracted me from the rest of my thoughts because it sounded like I had a missed message. I unlocked my phone to see that my cousin had texted me some time ago, and I'd never answered her back. Judging by the time of the sent message. It must have been during the time I was downstairs.

How was dinner?

It was bomb.

What all did you eat on your tacos?

I went for a taco salad

instead of traditional tacos.

Jessica simply replied, "*Oh.*"

The conversation between us bounced back and forth between tacos, what we were both doing at the moment, and the usual spiel on how terrible school was. We were equally excited for graduation that year, and our dreams were somewhat similar. We both wanted to get out of the town we had grown up in and go out on our own, and we both had big goals that we wanted to accomplish in our lives. We both wanted to get married and start a family, too. Jessica wanted to have a boy and a girl, and I was still undecided about if I wanted one of each or just all girls—although, we were both smart enough to know who really decided the sex of the baby.

Our conversation droned on and on until there became equal silence between the both of us, signaling we had run out of things to say to each other, and from here on out, random things would be spoken. Eventually, the random conversations died down, and I was left in total silence except for what was being played on my TV. The silence reminded me of how shallow and sad my life was to not have a life outside of home and school. I was soon encased in total boredom and depression at the same time.

I heard the door downstairs slam, letting me know that someone had either entered or exited our home. A few minutes later, I heard what sounded like a stampede, which caused my room to shake. I didn't know what the hell was going on, but at that moment, I didn't care. Another minute went by, and I received a text from my mother: *Your grandfather is here.* I quickly replied that I was on my way down and sat the phone next to me face-side down.

I lay there looking up at the ceiling with my hands across my chest, not really feeling anything at all. I was just taking in all the silence around me and wondering how long I should be up there before my mother texted me again. After a few minutes of looking up at the ceiling, I decided it was time to go downstairs and grace my grandfather with my presence.

I made it down to my sister's room and I could already hear the commotion coming from the downstairs kitchen between my sister, Raven, and my grandfather. It sounded like the girls were keeping him busy. Trying to keep quiet,

I slowly made my way down the stairs too. But the old stairs couldn't keep a secret even if they wanted to.

I made it down to the first floor, and Devon was still in the living room, which was now encased in total darkness except for the TV. I wasn't sure if he was asleep or not, but I kept it moving.

I walked into the kitchen, and my brothers, my sister, and Raven were all surrounding Granddad at the kitchen table, which now had a beautifully decorated cake sitting in the middle of it. Everyone looked up from the delicious-looking cake, and all heads turned in my direction.

Granddad spotted me first and said loudly, "Hey, Teenie Weenie. Happy birthday."

For as long as I could remember, he'd always called me "Teenie Weenie," a nickname he'd made up for me when I was born since I was so tiny. It always made me blush to hear him call me "Teenie Weenie." I didn't know why, but I often found myself trying to hide my smile.

Raven, who'd never heard him say it out loud, burst into her little giggly laugh. She was so stinking cute that I shook my head and walked over to the table to join the rest of the family. Mom asked me if she should put candles on the cake. I said no, but the look of heartbreak that cast over her and Granddad's faces insisted that I should have at least one to blow out and make a wish. So, I gave in and let Mom grace my cake with one candle.

Judging by the look on Mom's face, she was so proud of this cake. She'd been practicing for years, since my thirteenth birthday, to perfect cakes. She even took a job where she could learn how to decorate them. When she wasn't working, she was practicing at home with her own icing. Pretty soon, she started watching videos on YouTube and other social media websites for how to make the perfect cake, inside and out. She'd bought a complete kit of all the tools she'd need for piping icing onto a cake, as well as shaving off the top layers of cake to make it look more professional.

Looking at my cake, I could tell she did exactly that—piped out icing from a bag, complete with decorations, after shaving the cake down. Who would have known that my mom's real passion was making cakes? Pretty soon, she was displaying her art on Facebook for friends and family to see. The accolades she was getting made my mother proud, and some days, she was a changed woman because she was actually starting to get orders from people who saw her art on social media, and she finally had something she felt gave her purpose in the world.

After Mom put the single candle on my birthday cake, she left the kitchen and headed for the living room to ask Devon if he wanted to come and sing "Happy Birthday" to me. I don't know why on Earth she asked that man to present himself on my birthday. I ignored the very thought of him standing behind me as Mom turned off the lights and started singing. Devon's voice was loud, and it projected over everyone else's around me. I don't know if it was something he did on purpose to annoy me or if it was because he was always that loud.

I could see Raven inching closer to my cake because she was readying herself to blow out my single birthday candle. The look of evil was upon her little red face from smiling so hard. When the song was over, she quickly thrust herself forward to blow the single candle out. I raced her to the finish line, and we both ended up blowing out my candle. She started her usual little giggle and clapped like it was all for her. I couldn't help but smile back at her because even though this wasn't her moment, I wasn't going to deny her.

A piece of me felt a little embarrassed to have the birthday song sang to me. Part of me felt I was a little too old. Hell, I was too old for everything else when it came to my mother, so I guess that mentality was starting to follow me in all aspects of my life. I knew I shouldn't be feeling this way. After all, I was only eighteen. This was supposed to be the beginning of a new me, a new life, and here I was feeling too old for a birthday song.

I got what I wanted for my birthday that year, and I couldn't ask for more. So, why did I have this embarrassing feeling? I tried to muzzle my smile by closing my lips over my teeth, and I placed my hand over my now-grinning face.

When the lights came back on, everyone laughed and cheered for me. Devon, of course, retreated to the living room while shouting behind him at my mother to bring him a piece of cake. My inner sassiness came out quickly enough for me to roll my eyes and let out a sigh before my mother could hand me the knife to cut it. I turned back to look at her in surprise because I'd never been put in charge of cutting a cake before, let alone my very own. I looked down at the knife before taking it from her hands and asked if she was sure.

Mom told me yes and that she wanted to see my face when I cut into it. My thoughts traveled back to earlier when I noticed the cakes on the stove cooling down. With all the colors she had baked, I wondered if it was my face she wanted to see or if she just wanted to be proud of the creation she'd made. I stood up from the table because this was a big moment, and I needed to get the right angle if I was going to do this correctly. As I put the knife to the cake, Mom shouted, "Wait!" and walked over to grab her phone from the sink.

A light flickered on from the back of the phone, signaling that she was now filming this moment. I was nervous about what my mother had done to this cake that had her filming it now. As I cut into the cake, Granddad made his usual left-handed joke and said maybe I should try and cut with my right hand. I grinned and concentrated on the task at hand so I wouldn't mess it up. But when I went to cut the other side of the oval-shaped cake, I noticed that it wasn't turning out so well. The slice of cake was way too big and not even close to being a perfect triangular shape.

Granddad looked over at Mom and said, "That piece is big enough for at least two people."

I felt the pressure and embarrassment of messing up my own cake settling in. I looked up at Mom with deer eyes, unsure of what to do next. She looked at me with excitement and told me to lift it up. Scared of what might come out of this cake or how jacked up it now looked, I reached over for a paper plate to throw this massive, jagged-looking piece of cake onto. It was so huge that the knife could barely hold it. So, I quickly threw the plate under the knife and cake, and I scooped the slice onto it. It was literally a rainbow cake, complete with all the colors, with thin layers of cream cheese icing between each layer.

I looked down at the giant piece of cake before me on the limp paper plate that was now struggling to hold it and wondered who would share this with me. It had become evident very quickly that everyone around the table wanted their own piece of cake. Mom was standing behind me with her camera recording how the cake looked on the inside before anyone else took a chunk out of it. After she was done recording, she took the knife and said she wanted to get in there and get Devon a piece really quickly before I started cutting. I rolled my eyes at the thought of her serving him before the kids simply because he told her to.

Mom handed the knife back to me.

"Who all wants some cake?" I asked.

In an uproar, everyone at the table wanted a piece, even Granddad—although, he said he shouldn't because his sugar hadn't been so good lately. I terribly cut pieces of cake for everyone.

Then I turned to Granddad and asked, "Do you trust my left hand to cut a piece of cake?"

He laughed and said, "Yes. Just don't make it as big as yours."

I tried my best to cut the smallest piece I could without having him complain, but I failed because it turned out to be too small.

"Do you want me to add onto it?" I asked.

"That's okay, Sugar." He said as he reached out for the plate.

Ashamed that I'd made his piece so small, I threw a fork on there. He finished it in just a few minutes while everyone else, including me, was still working on theirs. The boys finished theirs in record time in a hurry to get back up to their paused game, and Raven, well…

Did I mention she was two? Just like a toddler, her cake ended up all over her face, and she lit up with pride over it. At some point, she gained the attention of everyone at the table, and she turned it into a funny moment by smashing her face into her own plate and covering the rest of her face with the remainder of her piece of cake. Pretty soon, she was covered from chin to hairline and loving every minute of it.

"You're going to get in trouble if we don't get you cleaned up," I told her.

That triggered her, and she immediately stopped laughing.

"It's okay. I'll help you," I said as I walked her into the kitchen bathroom.

The water basically thinned and smeared the icing, making it harder to clean up her face. So, the task was becoming more and more frustrating. Frantic to clean her up before Mom heard the water running or her father came in demanding to know what happened, I started wiping her face in hopes that a little more force would remove the icing faster. After a while, her face was much cleaner—except for her hair, eyelashes, and the little bits of icing stuck up her nose. This just seemed too impossible, and at that moment, I was glad I didn't have any kids. After a little while longer, the evidence of cake face was completely gone.

I let Raven loose and sent her on her way. She quickly ran back to my sister and asked if she was ready to go upstairs to watch TV. God, the love that girl had for my sister was astronomical. My sister stopped her conversation with Grandfather like she was being rudely interrupted by her own kid, looked over at Raven and said, "Not yet." My sister loved her grandfather because he treated her like the princess she swears she is, and sadly, it almost always works.

Raven had the same exasperated look on her face as she did earlier during dinner. That poor child wanted nothing more than attention, and I wished I could give it to her, but she only wanted it from a select few—her mother, her father, and my sister. I'd offered for her to come up to my room to watch TV, but that lasted all of five seconds when she got bored and ditched me, saying, "I'm going to see what your sister is doing." I'll never forget that day. She stormed out of my room so fast to get downstairs, but it took her all of five minutes to get down twelve steps carefully.

I laughed at the thought of it, but then it quickly faded away when I noticed that my sister was hogging Granddad in hopes of getting something on my birthday. So, I sat down to regain his attention, and it worked because he looked over and asked, "How does it feel to be old?"

I smiled and said, "The same as yesterday."

He chuckled and then continued our conversation, not saying anything to include my sister, which quickly frustrated her to the point of grabbing her phone, throwing away her plate, and heading upstairs.

As she walked out, she said, "Bye," without looking back.

Granddad responded with grandfatherly love, and without missing a beat, he continued. "How was your day?" he asked me.

"The usual. I went to school this morning and then came home and took a nap until dinner. I just showered before cake, and now I'm here with you." I think the only thing he heard was *nap* because for the rest of the visit, he talked about how he'd taken so many naps earlier in his rocking chair.

"Same old Granddad," I said to myself, shaking my head.

After he finished his usual conversation, he looked down at his phone, signaling that it was time for him to go. He was retired, but he still liked to go home to do his daily chores before bed. He grabbed his phone and leaned in to kiss me on the forehead. He thanked me for the cake and said goodnight.

"Do you want some cake for later on tonight?" I asked.

"No, I'd better not with my sugar." But his eyes told a different story. He'd struggled with his weight, just like I had, and ever since he'd found out he was diabetic, I never pushed the issue of him wanting more.

As he headed towards the front door, I could hear him say goodnight to Mom and Devon, and then he was gone. Grandpa being present was my gift, although my sister had tried to pimp him for her own reward.

I sat there looking at the massive, half-eaten cake before me, and I wondered how I was going to put it away. I was now officially eighteen years old, and I found myself yelling to my mom from the kitchen, asking her what I should do with the rest of it. She yelled back for me to just leave it where it was because she had no idea herself about where she was going to put it. Looking in the fridge, I felt like this was almost a bad idea because there was literally no place for it.

I grabbed the half-eaten slice of cake that was still on my plate and headed back upstairs to my room. On my way up, I stopped to thank Mom for my birthday dinner and cake.

"How did I do on the cake?" she excitedly asked.

I smiled. "You did a good job."

She smiled back, and Devon interrupted the moment with, "Yeah, you did a good job, baby."

I rolled my eyes as nausea started to set in, and I turned to head back upstairs.

When I entered my sister's room, it was no surprise that the first thing to hit me in my face was the smoke built up from her doing her hair again. I rolled my eyes and thought, *One day, her hair is going to fall off from all that damn straightening.*

Raven, of course, was comfortable in her spot, sitting straight up, bright-eyed and bushy tailed, watching the

Disney Channel. She didn't even turn to look in my direction when I entered the room. That girl loved her some Disney Channel and wouldn't even flinch at the thought of someone being next to her when it was on.

I opened the door that divided our rooms and headed back up to my sanctuary. I walked inside the door and closed it behind me, looking up only to realize that I hadn't turned on the lights in my room. Cursing myself for not doing so, I wondered if I could make it up all twelve stairs without breaking my neck, even though the light switch to the attic was just a hand motion away from me. Stupid or trying to be brave—I didn't know which just yet—I decided to climb the stairs up to my room in complete and utter darkness.

I felt my way around in the dark like I'd lost my sight completely. I counted my way up the stairs, careful not to miss one so I wouldn't stub my toe or hurt myself. The thought of making it all the way up the stairs was such a thrill until I psyched myself out and thought, *What if there's a monster in my face right now and I don't even know it? I've got to stop watching scary movies in the dark because now I've scared myself into searching for the light when I was close to the very top.* The light on my TV screen gave me the confidence I needed to pursue this till the end.

I was on the last step when I suddenly changed my posture and lost my balance. Luckily, I regained my footing, shook my head at the thought of what could've happened, and entered my room by moving the fitted sheet aside and walking into the darkness. I needed to quickly turn on the lights.

"Boy, I really need to stop watching scary movies at night," I mumbled. "Once again, I'm grown, and I'm letting these movies get to me for no reason, especially when I know they aren't real."

I quickly flicked on the light, and the feeling of instant relief hit me as I looked around the room for confirmation that my birthday was officially almost over, and I couldn't even say, other than my birthday dinner and cake, that it was a good one. It was sad how I had no life or friends to spend days like this with. I was sure that if I had friends, they would have gone all out for me…just like I'd seen at school.

I had to be born a loner and an ugly, fat one at that. The thought of this put me in a depressive state for the rest of my birthday, and soon I rolled up into fetal position and fell fast asleep. I awoke later, feeling the fullness of my bladder and thinking, *I have the world's smallest bladder to have to pee so much.* The thought annoyed me, and I tried my hardest to ignore it and go back to sleep, but I couldn't…now that my body knew that I had a full bladder that needed to be emptied.

I lay there for a moment to try and ready myself for my departure downstairs. My TV was still on, so with its guiding light, I reached over to my nightstand to tap on my phone, bring it to life, and see what time it was. It was only just after midnight. I let out a deep, exasperated sigh, rolled over onto my back, and looked up at the ceiling. I was disappointed that my birthday was officially over, and I had slept the last few hours of it. I didn't know why I was disappointed in myself anyway. I made myself go to sleep when I got depressed over not having anyone to celebrate my becoming an adult with.

When the feel of my overly full bladder became too overwhelming, I decided it was finally time to make the trip downstairs. I rolled out of bed like a decrepit old person and felt around for my slippers with my eyes partially closed. Once I slipped the second one on, I scooted around my bed and slowly walked towards the exit. This time, I reached for the light to make my way downstairs. The light jolted to life, lighting the way down the stairs. I squeezed my eyes tightly, so it looked like I was squinting.

Reaching for the doorknob that opened the dividing door to my sister's room, I halfway expected to still see her and Raven wide awake as usual, my sister doing her hair for the millionth time and Raven sitting up, watching the Disney Channel. I wasn't expecting them to be asleep and cuddled up against each other. Raven's head was tucked under my sister's chin, and her body was pressed against my sister's body in fetal position.

Just like mine, their TV was still on as well, playing some random show on the Disney Channel. They looked so precious when they were asleep yet still so evil at the same time. I opened her bedroom door, not shocked to still hear my brothers playing their video game, which they'd probably play well into the morning. This made me roll my eyes because it was a school night, and they seriously played that damn thing until the sun just barely peeked its way through the darkness. But I had to give it to them—no matter what, they still managed to make it to school on time.

I headed to the bathroom, not even bothering to turn on the lights, because the nightlight by the sink was plenty of light for me. I did my business, was out of there in two minutes flat, and made my way back up to my room. Once I was back in my warm, body-imprinted spot, I fell fast asleep in no time, which came as a surprise since it usually took me a while to fall back to sleep during one of my bathroom breaks. I decided to leave the TV on because the soft murmur in the background kept me at ease.

Chapter 11
Graduation

The existence of snow was long gone, and as the warmth of a beautiful spring breeze crept its way in, there was a change in the atmosphere as graduation drew near. The excitement was contagious as the thought of graduating became very real. The very thought of being adults and moving onto a bigger and better place was on the eager minds of every young boy and young girl.

I, for one, couldn't wait to graduate. My plans were mine and mine alone. But the very thought of them made me nauseous, most days, because the idea of leaving this state was both thrilling and scary at the same time. I wanted nothing more than to live a life of my own, but when I thought about living miles away from a family, who hardly felt like my family, confusion set in.

There were a lot of *who, what, when,* and *where* questions going on in my head, when this time was supposed to be nothing more than a joyous occasion. Like, who was going to take care of my siblings when I was gone? Because, let's face it, our mom had other priorities than being a loving and devoted mother. What would they do without me? I'd done just about everything for them since birth. I'd cooked, cleaned, mediated during fights, and nursed when someone got hurt. But then again, I guess that's what big sisters are for, even though I was always the first they'd call or go to, even when Mom was around.

Then there was the bigger questions weighing heavily on my mind: When would I actually leave? And where would I go? Should I leave right after graduation, or should

I stay around for a little while? Where in the hell would I go?

I'd always said that if I were to run away from home, I would go to Seattle, and every time I was asked, "Why Seattle? Because of *Fifty Shades of Grey,* or just because you like rain?" My response was always the same to whomever asked, "I don't know. I just think it's pretty, and I don't mind the rain much compared to snow."

All of these questions made it nearly impossible for me to feel excitement for the future. When I should have been happy about graduating and being one of the first in my family to walk across the stage and beat teenage pregnancy, all I could think about was my siblings and what would happen to them when I finally up and left for good.

The thought of staying in the town where I was born and raised was depressing, especially when I felt like I was never going to leave. Other than my siblings, there was nothing left there for me. So many bad memories from when I was growing up outweighed the good, and they made it harder to think about what I had accomplished in my eighteen years on this planet. When I thought about it, I had nothing to show for my life. I couldn't remember one good memory as a child that would make me want to stay there any longer than I had to.

When the last bell of the day rang, drawing me out of my dazed and depressed state, I took the opportunity to walk home slower than usual to think heavily on this important decision to leave everything I knew behind after graduation. Upon exiting the century-old brick building, the thought of actually leaving the town where I was born and raised hit me hard. As crazy as it may sound, there were times when I didn't feel like I was a part of my family at all. I didn't feel that close bond to my siblings like the families on TV, and I didn't feel close to my mother at all most days.

It was crazy to think (or it was just me being paranoid) that one time when I really pissed off my mother, and she took it out of hand due to her bipolar disorder, she told me that sometimes she wished I was never even born. That memory hit me like a freight train. During one of our many arguments, I even brought it back up to see how she would react to what she'd said that broke me. She replied that she would never have said anything like that. But she did, and she had no idea how much it broke me to hear my own mother say those words and for her to not even remember or take ownership of saying something she couldn't take back—not even if she wanted to.

Boy, don't I feel stupid, I thought. *Here I am, worried about how my family will handle me leaving them after high school for a fresh start, and one family member wishes I was never born, and other days I feel like I'm not even part of this family.*

The thought of leaving my dysfunctional family made me feel nothing but guilt when in reality, they probably couldn't care less if I was there or not. On bad days, which were many, I found myself saying that I was only put here on this Earth to do what my mother couldn't and to be bullied and humiliated by my own family when it suited them.

The crisp, cool breeze of spring snapped me out of my self-pity. As I walked down the sidewalk towards the old cemetery, I stole a moment to close my eyes and soak up the beautiful breeze and take in the smell of spring. I could hear the sound of cars whizzing past me on the street, and a buzzing sound jolted my eyes in fear of it being a bee. But it must have already flown past me because I didn't see a bee or fly in sight.

The strong breeze blew my shoulder-length hair out of its resting place as I picked up the pace and walked past the cemetery. I didn't know what it was about cemeteries or hearses, but I didn't like to be near them, and it always bothered me that my school was surrounded by two of them—one behind the cafeteria and one up the hill.

As I rounded the corner near the cemetery, I saw the courthouse, letting me know that I was close to home. As I walked past the cemetery, I wondered if any of the tombs' stones had my last name on it, seeing as this cemetery had been here for hundreds of years and there was bound to be a *Smith* over there somewhere. I quickly scanned through the names before me, and there was no *Smith* in sight. I couldn't say I recognized any of the other names, at least none that were close to my family members' names. I did, however, notice that the grass had recently been cut, which I found odd because apparently the city was still paying for a groundskeeper. But then again, I figured it was reassuring for the living to know that their loved ones' permanent home was being well taken care of.

I turned to look at the opposite side of the cemetery to cross the street when a car came speeding down the opposite direction. I shook my head in annoyance because the speed limit through there was twenty-five miles per hour, which the driver of that car was choosing to ignore. I looked both ways to see if the coast was clear before striding across the street.

Once I was safely across the street, I sneaked a peek at the other tombs that were identical to the ones across the street. Still no *Smith*. That name must not have been popular, or no one by that name settled in this town back then. Either way, it didn't bother me knowing that the most popular last name in history was not on a tombstone.

I felt my settled stride becoming a brisk walk down the hill as I approached yet another street I had to cross to get to my house. My stride down the hill was fast, bringing me to a quick halt at the stop sign just before crossing onto the next street. Bringing my right foot in to connect with my left on the sidewalk, I felt the need to take this moment to pause before walking up yet another hill. Walking downhill can take your breath away just as much as walking up, but luckily for me, my house was right in the middle of the next one.

As I took my moment to pause, I looked off into the distance and searched for where the music was coming from. It sounded like it was coming from the same direction as my house. I rolled my eyes and prayed that it wasn't *actually* coming from my house. The last thing we needed was to be known as the "loud ones" on this street, even though we were surrounded by a band of misfits.

I continued my journey to the top of the hill where the noise of loud music and jumbled-up conversations was unfortunately coming from; it was my house, after all. I saw my mom's car was there, but it was parked further from the house than usual, which meant she had either just gotten there, or someone who was in our house parked in her spot.

Despite the sound of chaos coming from my house, my soul was at ease knowing that my mother was there. I climbed the seven steps to my front door while trying to fish my key out of my Thirty-One bag.

I literally just threw the damn key in here this morning when I left the house for school, so why am I always fishing for it when I get home? I thought.

I threw pieces of my purse to the ground because, at that point, I didn't know how long I'd had it, but it was really starting to fall apart inside. I just couldn't bring myself to throw it away because it had my name embroidered on it, and I never bought myself things. Plus, it was one of the few things that was all mine.

I finally found my keys hiding under a few pieces of scrap paper with some names and numbers on it, making me wonder why I still had them and who they belonged to. "I should really start throwing shit away and not keep everything in sight," I said to myself as I stuck the key into the lock. I turned the key, only to realize that the door wasn't locked.

As I cracked the door open, the annoying noise escaped as I snaked my hand into the mailbox in search of today's mail. "Hmm, no mail," I mumbled, wondering if the mail had come yet or if it had already been grabbed.

I pushed the door all the way open and saw a man standing in the middle of the floor near the back, stomping his foot and waving a white towel around, not in rage but from excitement. I don't know what the hell they were talking about, and I didn't really care to know. I just wanted to get upstairs and stay there.

I walked inside and shut the door behind me, catching a glimpse of Raven on the couch watching her usual show, *Phineas and Ferb,* on the Disney Channel. *It doesn't take much to make that child happy*, I thought as a grin crept across the right side of my face.

As I turned from the door, I noticed the mail on the end of the coffee table. I quickly reached for it like I just knew there was something for me. I skimmed through the stack, not having any luck, until I saw a letter for me from my school. It was addressed to me and my parent or guardian. In fear that it was about something I may have done in school, which might have gotten me in trouble, I shoved the letter in my old, mangled purse and rushed past the TV while saying hello to Raven, as I slipped past her. She paid me no mind, and she didn't say anything back to me. She was too caught up in her show to even notice that I was there.

The guy who was once standing in the middle of our floor and marching to the beat of his own drum was now excusing himself out of my way.

Oh, he's cute. He's light-skinned with what looks like blue eyes, and if I'm not mistaken, he's a ginger. Very cute.

The sound of my mother's voice broke my curious gaze away from this beautiful specimen in front of me. "Hi, Toza! How was school?" she asked me.

"It was alright." I turned my head quickly enough to reply before heading upstairs but not before Devon stole the moment by mimicking what my mother had just said in his girly voice.

"Hi, Toza," he whined.

His voice sent chills down my spine. This man knew that I despised him, yet he still made a point to annoy me at any given chance. I didn't even bother to turn around and give him the satisfaction of seeing the pissed look on my face. I just continued up the stairs as I replied in my most annoying tone, "Hi, Devon" just to avoid the argument for which my mother would purse her lips if I didn't say anything back.

Before I even reached the last stair, I could hear that my brothers were already home, judging by their choice words over their video game. And my sister was presumably burning the hell out of her hair right now. I cracked the door wide enough to stick my head in and say, "Hi," to my brothers. Without breaking their gazes from the TV screen, they responded, "Hi," in unison. I shook my head and laughed at them for being so into their game that they didn't even make eye contact.

As I walked over to my sister's door, the smell of burnt hair was in the air, and it almost choked me. I turned the knob and instantly regretted it. I was immediately hit by the all-too-obvious smell of damaged hair, as smoke escaped into the hallway. Her hair literally couldn't get any straighter, and the fact that she insisted on straightening it every day was maddening.

"Jesus," I said. "At least turn it down a few notches, why don't you, before you burn your hair off your scalp."

She pretended not to hear me, as she continued pulling the straightener down her long strands of hair.

"Okay," I said, as I opened the door, letting the smoke sneak its way into my room.

I flipped the light switch, lighting my way up the stairs. Once I'd gained access to my room, I flipped the switch again, turning off the light. Like climbing that hill every day after school, those damn stairs were a constant reminder of how much I truly needed to lose weight. I sat my purse down on the bed and immediately kicked my shoes off, as if my feet were on fire. I hated wearing shoes, not to mention clothes, so my pants came off next, as they were thrown onto the edge of my bed.

Once I was in my most comfortable state, I eyeballed the curious letter shoved into my purse. I scanned the front again as if I were looking for something that I may have missed before swiping it from the coffee table. I quickly scanned the back for any evidence of what it was, but I found nothing, so there was only one way to find out. I slid my pointer finger across the inside of the envelope, tearing it perfectly as if my finger were a letter opener. I quickly pulled the paper out of it and began to read.

The letter was from my school, letting me know that my SAT/ACT scores were both low. Dumbfounded about when I actually took these tests, I looked at the letter, and then I remembered they had us take them back when we were juniors. A whole damn year later and these test scores were just now being released, letting me know how significantly dumb I actually was.

Great. There goes my whole plan to actually leave this damn town. I reread the letter in search of something that I might have missed. *Nope. I'm officially dumb.*

All the doubt I'd put inside my head about not leaving this place out of guilt had led up to this very moment where reality was telling me I wasn't going anywhere at all. *How in the hell am I supposed to get into college with low SAT/ACT scores?* I silently lamented. *The answer is you can't. No college will accept anyone who has low scores. I just screwed myself and my future by not taking this damn test seriously when I had the chance to take it. I know they said before the test that our scores could impact wherever we went from here, but I didn't think they were serious.*

Unsure of where to go from there, I spiraled into a depressive state. The thought of being stuck there forever was starting to look very real and very sad for my future. All I'd ever wanted was to get away from this toxic life I'd lived and to never be anything like my mother when I finally had a little family of my own. Now, I wasn't so sure how any of this was going to happen if I couldn't make a future for myself.

I snatched up the empty envelope and the life-altering letter and threw them into my waste basket. I said to myself, *It's just a test and it doesn't define who I am, but let's be honest—I just BS'd on my whole future in three hours.*

The room started spinning, and I was dizzy over the thought of screwing up my life. I shook my head, trying to remove all doubt, because I was determined to get the hell out of there one way or another.

    I removed the rest of my clothes in a fit of rage, determined to take a shower in hopes that the beat of the cascading water would calm my spirit. Once I was fully naked, I grabbed my towel, which was hanging on my vanity mirror, and wrapped what I could around me. I swung open the curtain that acted as a bedroom door and flipped the switch, bringing the lightbulb to life above. I still hated walking barefoot on hard floors, and the stairs leading up to my room were so damn old they had loose nails sticking out, but my rage made me ignore all of that.

    I almost ran down the stairs when I realized I sounded like Big Foot, and judging by the look on my sister's face, she thought so too. But I was too upset to acknowledge my sister's annoyed face, so I grabbed the door handle and swung the door back, telling myself not to slam it or my sister's mouth would be open for all to hear. I almost made good on the promise, but not quite, although if I'd really unleashed my anger, it would have been worse for the old door.

    I was lost in my rage when I slammed the bathroom door, and I realized that I was now dizzy from all the quick movements I just did to get down there. I threw myself against the back of the bathroom door and pushed it completely shut, so it would take a bit of muscle to get it open now. I took a moment to let the room stop spinning and calm myself down before I walked over and turned on the shower, giving myself time to relax even more while the water heated up. When the steam started to encircle the corners of the mirror, I knew it was time to get in, so I grabbed my washcloth, hung my towel on the handle by the shower, and entered. Allowing the hot water to hit the front of my body first, I slowly stepped into the steaming stream of water so it was up to my neck, almost touching my chin.

The water was hot—almost too hot—but bearable and at the perfect temperature for my back. It was almost like my own personal spa as the steam surrounded my naked, wet body.

I almost wanted to tilt my head back and let the hot spray take over, but I wasn't ready to wash my hair yet. I fought the temptation to be swallowed up by the falling water. And just like that, the thought of failing myself and my future just faded away and ran down the drain. I felt contentment and not so much shame and anger anymore. I closed my eyes and let the cascading water envelop me as I massaged the soap into my skin. "God, I love Dove bodywash," I said to myself as the smell of the soap filled the room.

I was almost done when I realized I haven't been in there long enough to really let my worries melt away, so I slowly washed a second time. By the time I'd completely washed my full body from head to toe, I knew I'd been in there for a little over twenty minutes, judging by the lack of hot water that was now merely lukewarm. It was a temperature that was acceptable for babies but not for adults, so I rinsed the rest of the soap off and fully stood under the water a moment longer, allowing the rest of the hot water to fade away.

I knew that within the next half hour to an hour, the water would be scalding hot again for the next person to shower, but since it was still early in the day, the next shower wouldn't be until nightfall. And I could say with certainty that it wouldn't be my brothers to shower next. They made it a point to shower in the morning before school—that was if they got up on time. Other than that, it was between my sister, Mom, and Devon, and since everyone was busy doing their own thing, that water had plenty of time to heat back up.

The cold floor made me feel like I needed to step back into the shower where it was warm and clean, but I made haste with my towel around the rest of my wet body and headed for the door after washing and rinsing off. I pulled, hoping the door would spring open, but it jerked out of my hand, reminding me that I'd completely closed it earlier when I ran in there during my fit of rage over the disappointing letter. So, I stood like I was getting ready to battle, put my back into it, and pulled. The door loudly jolted open, and it drew attention from downstairs.

Embarrassed that I had just done that, I ran to my sister's door when I heard Devon say from downstairs, "Oh, it's just Toza." *Great.* Now he'd just seen me running from the bathroom half-naked since the towel only covered half of my fat ass.

The cold, displaced tiles against my semi-dry, clean feet put a pep in my step, and I moved faster upstairs to my room. I almost moved like I was being followed but not chased because the water from the rest of my body was now travelling down to my ankles and feet, and I feared that if I attempted to run, I just might fall.

I finally reached the comfort of my own bedroom after having dodged burnt hair, loose nails, and lifted floorboards. My heart was pounding so hard I could feel it in my chest. With each beat, I could feel the pressure slowly rise in my head and ears along with the smell of stress sweat coming on. I tried to calm myself down before full-on stress sweat made me head back downstairs to take another now-cold shower, so I dropped my towel to the floor to let the rest of my body air out and started taking deep, calming breaths while raising my arms between inhales.

It worked and I started to calm down, but the faint smell of stress sweat was still in the air, so I decided to turn on my air conditioner to help the rest of the smell dissipate. If I could get my body temperature under control, I figured I might be able to save myself from having to take another shower and just "bird bath" the affected areas. I stood completely naked in front of my air conditioner with my legs and arms spread wide to make sure every curvature of my body was cooled down before getting dressed.

After a few minutes with the air on full blast, I felt as if I could get dressed. The smell of stress sweat was a thing of the past. I couldn't even tell which parts of my body were affected and which parts weren't. When it came to hygiene, that was one thing I wouldn't take chances on.

I put on a pair of my pajama shorts and a tank top and then sat on the edge of my bed to give myself a few moments of peace before I headed back downstairs to see what was in the kitchen to drink. I usually brought a bottle of water upstairs with me before retreating to my room until dinner, but in all of the chaos, I decided to skip the kitchen and head straight upstairs. But now, I slipped on my favorite pair of black flips flops that I bought a couple years ago when Old Navy was having their annual Black Friday sale. They were worn down a little because they were all I wore to and from school when the weather permitted, but they were still comfortable.

Now that I was calm and in a better place, I found myself trying to be extra quiet coming down the stairs and heading into my sister's room. She was still doing her hair in the same spot she'd been for the last two hours. She'd gone from straightening her hair to trying different hairstyles. I noticed that the straightener was still on, but at least it wasn't in her hair. *Talk about heat damage.*

I headed out of her room and stopped at the bathroom. I wondered if I should go ahead and do myself a solid by giving myself that little bird bath now to make sure there were no signs of my earlier stress sweat before I went all the way downstairs. The last thing I wanted to do was smell bad in front of Mom and Devon's friends. I couldn't care less about Devon and what his friends thought, but then I would have to hear it from Mom, and she found any and everything embarrassing to talk about, no matter who was around. She did her best damage when her friends were with her, so I decided to slip back into the bathroom this time and not give her any opportunities.

Praying it had been long enough for the water to heat back up, I went to the sink and turned the knob for the hot water. It sprang from the faucet, cold at first, putting me back in full panic mode that it hadn't had time to heat up just yet. Then it slowly started to get warmer and warmer until it was hot, so I grabbed my already-damp washcloth and threw it in the sink long enough for me to take off my shirt and toss it in the bathroom closet.

I grabbed the wet cloth from the sink and instantly dropped it back in. I winced at how hot the water had gotten and quickly turned on the cold water to balance it out, putting my hand under the faucet every few seconds to test the temperature between each turn of the knob. Finally, it was at the right temperature, so I reached back in for the cloth and rang it out. I decided to add a little soap from the bar sitting on the sink just to make sure I was covering all my bases.

I wiped under my neck, each breast, and my armpits since those were the main areas where my body held sweat, especially under my neck. Once I was completely covered in soap, I let it set in for a minute to give it a chance to seep into my skin. I couldn't be too sure when it came to hygiene.

After a minute, I started rinsing the cloth under the water to get rid of the excess soap and started wiping off those three main areas. Once I was completely soap-free, I reached for a clean towel in the linen closet and started patting myself dry, careful not to miss any parts.

I tossed the towel on the floor at my feet and grabbed my shirt. I put it back on, picked up the used towel, and reached for the doorknob, praying it didn't jolt open like it had last time. It did, but this time it took less force. You couldn't sneak out of this bathroom even if you wanted to because the top of the door was split in two, making it catch against the doorframe when it was closed.

I slowly went down the stairs, careful not to draw attention to myself, cursing myself for being overweight when one step made a creaking sound. The sound swiveled the head of the beautiful man from earlier, who was stomping his feet and defeatedly waving a white towel. He looked to see who was coming in his direction.

Damn, I said to myself. I was wearing a tank top with no bra and my bedroom shorts, which I was sure he didn't wish to see on a big girl such as myself, not that he would be into me anyway. At first glance, he looked like he was into white women or women closer to his complexion, so for a brown girl like me—not a chance.

Mr. Beautiful stood up with a red cup in his hand that wasn't there earlier when I came in. It smelled of alcohol and looked dark, so my guess was rum or bourbon. He looked at me and raised his cup before saying, "Excuse me," and giving me a nod of appreciation or respect.

"Excuse me," I said as my foot touched the floor.

I ignored the smirk on Devon's face as he parted his lips once more and said, "Hey, Toza!" as if he were seeing me for the first time today.

I rolled my eyes and headed towards the kitchen when I heard his deep, dark laugh coming from the bottom of his throat. Mom was still doing some woman's hair. She was braiding it and looked like she was going to take a while.

I headed into the kitchen in search of something to drink. I walked over to the fridge and opened it. There were many options, but I was only in search of one thing—a bottle of water. It looked like there were only a few, so I gratefully grabbed one and closed the fridge. Quickly cracking the bottle open, I welcomed the cold stream of water down my throat. It was so good I found myself chugging until the coldness hit my back teeth and brought my big gulps to a halt for some relief and a breath.

I pulled the half empty bottle of water from my lips and let out a loud "ahhhh" in appreciation. I could still feel the coldness making its way down my throat. It was almost painful due to the amount that I'd just gulped at one time. I recapped the bottle and looked around the kitchen in search of something to snack on. Although I wasn't really all that hungry, the taste of the water had me wanting something savory or salty.

I looked in the cabinets and found a box of cake mix. I wasn't really in the mood to bake a whole cake, so I searched for something else that did not require baking or cooking because, by then, it was almost dinnertime. I looked in all the cabinets, freezer, and deep freezer, but I didn't find anything I wanted. Eyeballing the box of vanilla cake mix again, I thought, *If I bake this cake, I can turn it into cake balls. That way, we'll have dessert after dinner.*

I remembered how to make cake balls from the job that I'd just started a week after my eighteenth birthday at a behavioral health clinic as a behavioral health technician (BHT). I wanted a job so badly as a way to escape reality of all the responsibility I knew was waiting for me once I got home, and this one was mostly overnight, so the thought of having twelve hours away from life made things bearable.

I remained employed there a little over two years. I don't miss that place, at all, because I was stabbed in the neck with a fork, and a client tried to rape me.

Excited to make something I learned at my new job, I searched for icing to piece it all together once it was done baking. I found the icing in the cabinet next to the box and preheated the oven to 350 degrees. I searched the kitchen for the rest of the ingredients, like two eggs and oil, that the cake called for.

I laid everything on the table and poured the mix into a bowl. I carefully followed the directions on the back of the box since it had been a while since I'd made a cake.

As I mixed the cake batter, I thought about the crazy adventures I'd had that year. *I can't believe I actually turned 18… And got my first job… And lost my virginity at a Halloween Party.*

Chapter 12
Not So Virgin Mary

The Halloween party wasn't so much of a party. It was in the basement of my cousin's house, and there was barely anyone there—no one to really call a friend. I'd worn black yoga pants that had holes in the thighs from constant friction and an old pink tank top because I didn't mind showing my arms around my cousin.

Initially, I was saving myself for marriage, but when one combines alcoholic drinks, things like that go out the window. To make matters worse, I was pretty sure I'd been in a threesome with a guy who had formerly gone to school with me and had graduated a couple of years before me and the other girl I was previously acquainted with. It wasn't the romantic fantasy I'd made up in my head of how and where I was going to lose my virginity. The whole thing was just sad, really. I couldn't even remember how it started. I just remembered being handed a cup and told to try whatever was in it. There was ten minutes of pain, and then the whole ordeal was over. I sobered up enough to drive home that night feeling like I had just been used because none of it was romantic. And the pain between my legs was enough to make me want to cry when I tried to pee right afterwards. I was told sex for the first time was painful and not pretty in the slightest, and they were right. Nothing was pretty about bleeding and having sore genitals for a few days.

After that night, I tried my hardest to steer clear of my mother because she used to say to her friends that if any of her kids were having sex, she would know just by looking at them because you got a certain kind of look when you'd had sex. I tried to avoid any and all contact with my mother for the next two weeks. I was afraid she might take one look at me and know right away what I had done.

Here we were in April with May around the corner. We were months away from October, and so far, I'd heard nothing yet about her suspecting that I was no longer a virgin. I vowed to myself after that night to never have sex again until marriage in hopes that I might be able to save myself for my future husband. Honestly, I was also unreasonable, thinking that one night may have ruined me for good because I'd heard stories of how guys can tell when a woman isn't "tight" anymore. If we're being honest, the guy who took my virginity was way above average in size. It honestly scared the hell out of me when he pulled it out of his pants because I thought there was no way it was going to fit inside me.

After multiple attempts and failures, trying to get it in, he finally succeeded. And boy, did it hurt like hell?! So, of course, I thought that after my one night with a well-endowed man, I was ruined for good and was no longer as tight as I was all those months ago. I was even afraid that I may have been pregnant when my period was a little late, but when it started, that concern ended. My now only concern was if the regular-sized tampon was going to fit or fall out, now that I wasn't a virgin anymore.

Needless to say, I worked myself up for no apparent reason after I lost my virginity. It made my paranoia have paranoia. I'm proof that you should save yourself for marriage and not let people get into your head when it comes to losing your virginity. I wished I'd done my own research before taking that big step into adulthood. *Sex isn't the same for everyone, nor should it be, so make it your own when you're old enough to enjoy it.*

Those thoughts of the past year were just that—in the past—and it was time to look forward to the future. For starters, how in the hell was I going to get out of this small town when my plan to go to an out-of-state college was now ruined?

I finished mixing all of the dry and wet ingredients and tossed the cake into the oven for baking. The box said twenty-five to thirty minutes, depending on the pan size, so I looked for a pan similar to the one on the box and started the timer on my phone. I cleaned up the mess I'd made and put away the clean dishes after putting the batter into the oven.

I stood in the kitchen wondering if I should go back upstairs since I had a timer on my phone that would let me know when the cake was ready, but then I remembered the blue-eyed beautiful man who had made our stairs his new home for the time being. I was already shy and embarrassed at the slightest attention any man gave me whether he was into me or not, and I didn't want him to have to keep getting up and sitting down just to let me by. So, I decided to get comfortable on the bench attached to our kitchen table for the next twenty-five minutes. Besides, cakes didn't really take that long to bake, so it wasn't like I'd be sitting there forever.

Once it came out of the oven, the cake still needed to cool, and I could go back upstairs for that. Grateful that I'd brought my phone down (even though no one contacted me other than my cousin and my mom), I filled the time with social-media surfing, looking at what my fellow peers were up to. There were so many pictures of fun-filled times and future plans for graduation before most of them were off to college.

I often wonder how my life would've looked if I had been born into a different family. Would it look like every day was a beautiful day, and every year was a trip to somewhere around the world?

Cousin Jessica was always telling me to be grateful because there were kids who were worse off and didn't have a family. Still, sometimes I felt like I didn't have a family either. But then I thought about the ones who were sleeping outside in the cold and terrible summers with no food to eat, and I was brought back down to reality. There were people worse off than this. It was just hard to see sometimes when it came to my family and my mom's choices in men.

Wallowing in my own pity again, I went over to check the cake as its sweet aroma filled the room. The timer was about to go off, so I hoped the sweet smell meant it was done baking. I pulled the oven door down to discover the cake was a beautiful golden-brown on the edges and a light tan in the middle. No toothpick or knife was needed to tell me it was finished baking.

I took out the cake and looked over it to make sure I didn't overcook it. I poked it here and there, and it was definitely finished. I sat it on the backburner to cool and turned to head back up the stairs.

As I left the kitchen, Mom asked, "What are you cooking? I can smell it."

"I just baked a cake to make cake balls," I told her.

"You're going to buy me another box because I needed that for a cake I was making for a birthday party."

"I'm sorry. I didn't know."

I turned on my heels to leave the room, but before I made it to the stairs, she asked, "What the hell are cake balls?"

"Mashed-up cake formed into a ball with icing."

I turned away just as the blue-eyed man got up from the stairs and headed into the kitchen. He was probably going to use the bathroom, but I was grateful I didn't have to ask him to get up again.

I ran up the stairs, leaving behind the discussion amongst the other adults in the room about what cake balls were. I made it safely back upstairs to my room and enjoyed the smell of cake in the air. I plopped down on my bed, grateful that it didn't cave in because of how old it was. "Boy, this damn thing sure is sturdy."

I found something of value to watch on TV while looking at the time on my phone to allow the cake to cool before I broke into it, and I hoped that by the time I went back downstairs, that beautiful man wouldn't be there. I lost track of time when another TV episode started, so I headed back downstairs, confident that I'd be able to safely walk down the stairs without having to interrupt Devon's friends.

I made it all the way down the stairs without having to ask for safe passage when I saw that the man was still there. He'd just switched places with the previous man who was sitting in the barber's chair.

Lord, how long has this man been here? I said to myself. *The woman who was sitting in Mom's chair is now gone, and Mom is in the living room watching Devon and the TV at the same time. It must get real exhausting keeping an eye on someone you so badly want to trust but can't.*

Mom made eye contact with me but didn't say a word, so I continued into the kitchen where my cake still sat on the back burner of the stove. I washed my hands and pulled it towards me, then laid my whole palm on it to check the temperature. It felt like it was the right temperature to break up and turn into cake balls. So, I opened the cup of cream cheese icing and started shredding the cake and mashing it into the pan. It was the right consistency now to start adding the icing, but I felt a moment of panic because I couldn't remember if I was supposed to add the whole container or only half. *God, if I screw this up, Mom will never let it go.*

I turned the icing container over and poured its contents into the cake pan. I looked at it once it was all poured in, and I instantly knew that I'd just fucked up, but it was too late to fix now. I couldn't put some of the icing back into the container because then it would be a mixture of icing and cake, and that would really piss Mom off.

I started looking around the kitchen for anything that would save the cake balls, but nothing came to mind. I looked at it and thought maybe it just seemed like a lot before I transformed them into balls.

It was evident that I had fucked up. The moment I tried to piece together the cake with the icing, it was clear that the pan was all icing and zero cake. My mom was going to lose her shit when she saw this. All I wanted to do was make a nice dessert for everybody to have right after dinner. Not only did I waste Mom's last box of cake and icing, but now I had to throw it away and tell her what I'd done. The only thing I didn't know was how much longer that guy planned on being here, and I wondered if I should just tell Mom now and let the embarrassment begin.

My hands were shaking. I had terrible butterflies in my stomach that were now turning into cramps, and my heart was racing. I headed into the living room, stood next to her on the side of the couch, and told her that I messed up the cake balls.

Mom didn't say a word at first. She just shook her head. Then she finally took a deep breath and said, "You didn't know what you were doing to begin with. You really owe me a new box of cake and icing."

I tried to defend myself and said, "I learned about it at work, but I just added too much icing when I shouldn't have."

"You didn't know what you were doing, and you wasted my stuff!"

The guy from the chair was now absent, and I decided to leave the living room before more was said. Wondering if he had heard all of that, I headed back to the kitchen to clean up my mess when he came out of the kitchen with a confused look on his face.

"Devon, what's that on the stove?" he asked.

Devon mumbled, "It was supposed to be cake balls, but she messed them up."

Great. As if it wasn't embarrassing enough for me to punish myself, now I had Devon adding more insult to injury. I quickly cleaned up the mess and threw away the ruined cake balls. I was ashamed to look at them in the trash and wondered if my mom was right about my not knowing what I was doing. Even though it had previously gone well for me at work, I couldn't explain what else had ruined it besides too much icing in a small pan. I could hear Devon and his friend, exchanging conversation about kids always messing up something. The conversation angered me even more since I wasn't Devon's damn kid, and he had every nerve.

I quickly washed up the dirty dishes and grabbed another water bottle out of the fridge because I intended on spending the rest of the night upstairs in my room. I figured I'd had enough embarrassment for one day. I left the kitchen the way it was before I entered it and power walked my way past Devon and his now smirking friend in the chair. I didn't even turn to look in my mother's direction because I was sure she was eyeing me all the way up the stairs.

I marched upstairs without missing a single stair, which is surprising because I usually get clumsy when I'm pissed off or humiliated. I entered my sister's room like she wasn't even there, made my way through the door, and slammed it behind me. Once back in my room, I cursed myself for letting Devon get under my skin. It was one thing when Mom did it because she either had an audience or she was having another bipolar moment, but this man, if that's what you can even call someone like him, did it for pleasure.

Devon knew none of my siblings liked him. He enjoyed doing spiteful, childish things to piss us off, which gave him great pleasure. I climbed into bed and grabbed my phone off of the nightstand. It should've had a full battery by now because I'd plugged it in before heading back downstairs. *Funny how I had to charge a phone that only two people called or texted me on.*

I turned my TV to the Food Network and spent the rest of the night upstairs. This wasn't the first night I'd gone to bed without dinner, and I was sure it wouldn't be my last. Eventually, I fell into a deep sleep and was lost in a serene dream about a bright, beautiful future and better days.

The last few weeks of school before graduation were filled with joy and heartfelt cries from those who had turned their friends into family. I, for one, was focused on just graduating. Having to enroll in community technical college instead of a university until my test scores became more appropriate was not ideal, but it was comforting to know that I was only doing this until I could get to where I needed to be. Besides, the best part was that all my bullies would be leaving this town, and I wouldn't have to endure being called a "cow" or "big nose" anymore.

The infamous "big nose" originated in elementary school and sadly made its course through my entire childhood and teenage years. But the worst was yet to come when the PCOS and diabetes diagnoses came. Growing up, Mom told me to *never* shave the facial or chest hairs, or they would grow back thicker, and I would be stuck shaving those areas for the rest of my life. Unfortunately, kids can be cruel, and if being picked on for having a big nose wasn't bad enough, try adding kids who didn't understand why a girl was growing facial and chest hair to the mix.

I never liked my body growing up; there was always some flaw that I didn't like about myself. For years, I looked like I was starving because I was a seriously active kid, but when we moved into a trailer park and were primarily surrounded by white kids, it was harder for me to continue to stay active. So, growing up in a house full of snacks and the constant eating of fast foods made it easier for a growing, extra-hormonal girl to gain weight at an unhealthy rate. The PCOS was just an added bonus to my already frustrating body, so in school and at home, kids made me hate my body even more.

The thought of suicide endlessly crossed my mind growing up, so much so that I thought of some gruesome ways to end it all—taking pills, slashing my wrists, sticking my head into the oven—but nothing ever seemed appropriate enough to get my point across. Plus, I knew I couldn't leave my family alone. Even at a very young age, my family was the center of my life, even though I wasn't theirs.

Back then, no one knew how depressed I really was. I was just seen as a child who needed to stay in a child's place. My opinions, my thoughts, and my voice didn't matter. As long as I was doing what I was told by my elders, no one cared about the rest. It was all just circumstantial to them. Mom knew of the bullies, and she did her due diligence and informed the families of the ignorant kids, but it just went in one ear and out the other for most. No one wanted to hear that their child was a bully, let alone believe it if they couldn't see it for themselves.

So, the bullying continued throughout my life, and my depression and negative feelings about myself weren't going anywhere anytime soon. That's why graduating meant so much to me until I found out I had no choice but to continue to call this place "home" for a little while longer.

I knew I wanted to invite both of my grandparents to my graduation because they'd been there for me the most growing up, which left me with three tickets. Of course, I had to invite my mother, even though I selfishly didn't want to, but what kind of daughter would I be if I didn't invite my own mother to my graduation, even if she was less than a mother behind closed doors? That left me with just two tickets. I had no one else I wanted to invite, so Mom suggested that I invite her longtime friend and my godmother, since Mom claimed that she was living with her throughout her pregnancy with me. That left me with just one ticket that I couldn't get rid of. I couldn't invite my cousin's mother because she was already going to be there for her, and anyone else I thought of either had plans or was invited to someone else's graduation. So that last ticket was trashed because there was no way in hell I was inviting Devon—or his kids.

That was it. I had almost everyone I wanted to invite coming to my graduation to see me ascend into adulthood.

The day before graduation was a wreck, but in the end, it was all too good to be true. Neither of my grandparents could make it, and my godmother was invited by another friend to see their child graduate. She was still going to be present, but she was no longer there just for me. I basically had no one there for me—no one other than the one person I hesitated giving a ticket to in the first place: Mom. But I knew if I didn't, she'd hate me even more than she already did. I wanted to cry because, even for one of the most important days in my life, I still had no one there for me.

Getting ready for graduation the next day didn't include all the bells and whistles I thought it would. I was now a "young woman," who was "gainfully employed," and I had nothing new to wear because I didn't have the money to go shopping, nor could I stop sweating long enough to do my hair.

Before I knew it, it was time to go.

Like being rushed out the door to catch the limo on your wedding day, all the excitement of it quickly faded as we drove away from the house. I was going to graduate. I would be the first in my family to graduate from high school, and I had no one in my corner who was going to be there for me other than the woman who'd brought me into this world.

The drive during the last hours of my childhood was filled with silence. Not even the radio could fill the empty space with sound. I looked out the window with regret in my eyes and a broken heart. Halfway there, Mom finally broke the silence with her version of trying to cheer me up by saying that I should be grateful because most kids had no one there for them today. A look of confusion crossed my face because I wasn't sure how she knew what I was thinking in that exact moment. But I knew she was right, and I acknowledged that, but at the same time, I also felt like one of those kids.

The closer we got to the university where the graduation was to be held, the heavier traffic got. Cars were filled with my classmates and their happy families. My family was late for everything in life no matter where we headed, and this day was no exception. I even made it into the bathroom early to get ready at home, but seeing the traffic now brought out the what-ifs. I knew we weren't late, but judging by the traffic, I couldn't help but think that we were.

Once we arrived and finally found an open parking space, the thought of having to hike all the way back to the university grounds in heels was not appealing. It made me regret my choice of shoe, but not being cute on this day wasn't an option.

Sweating out my freshly straightened hair multiple times before leaving the house and now walking all the way to the university annoyed me. I couldn't wait for this day to be over. Nothing seemed to be going right from my choice of clothes, shoes, and now my hair. Mom knew I was frustrated with my hair, and she chose that moment of all moments to remind me that she offered to curl my hair so it wouldn't look the way it did. Trying to keep my frustration in check, I ignored her. She knew my hair didn't hold curls well, so that was just her way of saying "I told you so."

Once we made it inside, we went our separate ways. I had to find my class, and she had to find seating. Once I found my class, I was urged to put on my gown. Of course, I'd just hiked a mile to get there, and I was sweating like a pig. Did I really want to put on this damn gown? But, I put it on, leaving it unzipped in the front for air to circulate through. We were all asked our sizes for our gowns, and looking at mine, I felt like I'd made a mistake. After seeing my classmates, I realized that I should have chosen a longer gown.

Great. So not only was I sweating my hair into an afro, but now it was also clear that my gown was a little bit shorter than everyone else's. It stopped right at the knee. Growing more and more frustrated as I compared myself to others, I felt that this was the worst graduation ever. Fanning myself with my hat to keep the sweat off my face, I heard my name and turned around in a swift movement. Some of my classmates were admiring my shoes and commending me on being able to walk in them. I thanked them and just like that, the group of girls who'd been friends since middle school walked away in the same fashion as they'd come.

The compliment brought a little smile to my face for a moment until I realized just how much these shoes were actually killing my feet. I looked around for somewhere to sit when one of our teachers walked in and started lining us up by last name.

Oh, my aching feet! What possessed me to think I could last long in these damn shoes?

After I took my place in the *S* section, I prayed she'd get through the rest of the alphabet faster and the grand old graduation march song would begin playing so I could sit. She got through the rest of the alphabet in record time and flew to the front of the line, signaling that we were ready to enter. The song started, and the line slowly began to shuffle into the overcrowded gym. All of the eager graduates took our seats to begin the commencement. Once we were all seated, I felt the need to relax, not just because I could finally rest my throbbing, sore feet, but also because this was *it* for all of us. I didn't have any real friends to be sad about not seeing anymore, but there would no more high school and only more of the rest of lives.

The last of the line was seated, the music stopped playing, and the principal took her place on stage to begin her farewell speech. In this moment, everything felt alive. *I* felt alive. I'd forgotten the last twenty-four hours of disappointment from family and felt nothing but pure happiness. This was the first time that I had felt my life was worth living. Knowing that I'd be the first to graduate in my family gave me something to look forward to.

The speech lasted a good ten minutes, and then it was time. Our names were being called. Grateful that my last name began with an *S,* I had a chance to look upon all the faces before me. Witnessing their excitement and joy gave me excitement and joy, too. I couldn't contain the cramps and constant fluttering in my stomach, but I didn't care because this was it.

I was graduating!

When it came to the *S*'s, I looked at my friend Marty, who was in front of me. I was jealous of him and how he somehow managed to still graduate with honors, despite his family having a house on the beach that they lived in every winter until summer break.

Our row was next to be called. The usher came by and told our row to stand. We stood there, eager, giggling, and full of light and excitement. One by one, we all lined up next to the stage and eagerly waited for our names to be called. I looked out at everyone in search of their excited faces and in search of my mother, who'd miraculously found a seat way in the back next to my godmother. The closer they got to my name, the stronger the butterflies fluttered in my stomach.

When I was next to be called, I laughed to myself because I just knew they weren't going to get my name right. No one had ever gotten my name right, so I just knew this time would be no different.

The principal looked down at the piece of paper that held all 250 students' names, looked up, and took a deep breath. "Tozaneé Shanteesé Smith."

There it was. She'd said my nam*e. Correctly!* The shock of her saying my name like she'd been saying it my entire life distracted me from the fact that the entire gym had erupted into screams and cheers for me.

They were cheering for me! They were all cheering for me like I was a popular cheerleader or the quarterback on the football field. I was confused and had a stupid grin on my face as I walked up to retrieve my diploma because I couldn't believe that they were all cheering for me. After shaking several hands and posing for a picture with my new diploma, I focused on not ruining the moment and falling face down on the podium in these God-forsaken heels.

That was it. I'd officially graduated, and the girl who spent her whole life being bullied and didn't have a person in this world to call a friend was just screamed and cheered for upon ascending the throne to adulthood. *What the hell was that about?* I thought.

I was so wrapped up in the excitement of being the first in my family to get a degree that the thought of what just happened soon faded away as the last of us took our seats. The principal returned to the microphone and signaled for us to turn our tassels to the left before the gym erupted once more into cheers of excitement and screams as we tossed our hats into the air for one final hoorah.

Chapter 13
The Beginning of an End

The rest of the day was full of total bliss and love, but my week would end in pain and deception. Two days after graduation, I got into yet another gut-wrenching argument with Devon over his immaturity. Mom quickly took his side and cast me out onto the street with nowhere to go. I called my cousin, and she helped me haul what I could in several big black trash bags, and I went to stay with her and her family. The pain was too much to bear because the thought of my mother actually taking the side of someone she didn't give birth to was too much to process, so I took a handful of my diabetic medicine and waited for the end to come.

I spent the next three days in the ICU. Having my stomach pumped and humiliating myself as well as my cousin and her family, I felt I had nothing left to live for. It turns out that taking 180 pills of Glucophage doesn't kill you, at least not as fast as I would have liked, but I was feeling the aftermath of it all. I was weak, and I had diarrhea for a week, but that was the least of my worries. Not only did I try to commit suicide and fail, but I also felt like the whole world knew, and any future I had for myself was gone.

My mother never visited me while I was in the ICU; however, she did come when I went to ER. She sent everyone else in my family to check on me and scold me for being so stupid instead. When the doctors were sure I wasn't going to die, they sent me down to the psych ward for further evaluation of my mental health. I hadn't eaten in over three days, and now I was being processed as a crazy person in a room to myself.

The nurse who checked me in displayed a rather large, fresh hickey on the side of her neck, and she was proudly displaying it with her hair pulled back for everyone to see. I looked around the room and glimpsed at all the other women who looked like they were in their early twenties or possibly still in high school. The nurse with the hickey on her neck was the only one who looked like she was old enough to work down there, and judging by the way she acted with the nurse who released me into her custody, she was still trying to hold on to her youth by acting like the younger ladies on her team—except they didn't have hickeys on their necks.

Every morning, a nurse would come in around 5:00 a.m. to check my sugar and to draw my blood for testing. My fingers were filled with so many holes they didn't have anywhere else to stick me. Looking and feeling hopeless, I just lay on the one-inch mattress they called a bed. We got three meals a day, but since none of mine were ever touched, it created concern for my health between the nurses and my doctor. I'd take a sip here and there of whatever beverage they placed in front me, but other than that, I had gone five days without a solid piece of food.

I couldn't stop feeling sorry for myself for stooping so low and doing something so stupid. The final words of my mother's voice when she came into the emergency room where I was being held until a room became available in the ICU still rang in my ears.

With looks of concern and disapproval in her eyes, she asked, "Was what you did worth it? Was it worth putting your cousin and her family through this? You think they're gonna welcome you back into their home after what you did?"

I looked away and said, "You need to leave."

I was scared that she was going to lash out after hearing those words exit my mouth, but she didn't. She just turned around and left. That was the last time I saw her until then.

After lunch, with my tray still completely full, I was told I had visitors. Surprised since I hadn't had visitors since I left the ICU, questioned who would be visiting me. Nurse Ratchet, who had another fresh hickey on her neck next to the one that was just starting to fade, walked me out to the visiting area. My mother and grandmother sat on a couch next to each other staring out into the open as if they were preparing themselves for this visit.

Nurse Ratchet sat me down and told us that I had ten minutes and no more than that. My mother handed her a grocery bag and claimed that there was some stuff inside for me. Nurse Ratchet took it and went back into the ward and closed the door behind her. There was a window in the ward where she could see me.

I looked up at the clock on the wall and watched the big hand move. *Ten minutes. Okay, let's see how long I can sit here before someone says something.*

No one said anything for what seemed like an eternity. Then the voice of my grandmother rang out. "How have you been?" she asked.

I didn't know how to answer that question since I was stuck here in a psych ward, so I just shrugged my shoulders and looked down at the floor. They both looked at each as if silently saying this was uncomfortable, so my mother finally said, "Don't you feel you should apologize to us for putting your family through this?"

Anger quickly filled my body along with tears threatening to fall from my eyes. Shaking, I looked at her and asked, "Why should *I* apologize when you spent years telling your friends that you would never take the side of a man over your own kids?" Tears rolled down my cheeks as I spoke.

Mom used to preach it like it was in the Bible, but she couldn't even answer my question directly without once again taking his side. "He is an adult, and you need to respect him."

This was true. He was an adult, and I should respect him, but it was also hard to do so when that adult acted more like a child than his two-year-old and didn't respect the kids of his current girlfriend, let alone her. But it was clear there was no getting through to my mom at this point. She still felt the need to take Devon's side, and here I was in a psych ward after trying to take my own life over her kicking me out of the house for him.

So, I stood and said, "We have nothing more to talk about."

I headed back to the door to reenter my current home. Nurse Ratchet buzzed me back in, and I turned to close the door behind me, taking in one last view of this dysfunctional family intervention.

Nurse Ratchet handed me the bag my mom brought in for me. There was a pack of new underwear, since I'd been walking around without a bra or underwear on, and two bags of peppermint and butterscotch candy. The pack of underwear was ripped completely open as well as the candy. Apparently, things needed to be searched before they could be given to us, which was understandable since we were in a psych ward.

I didn't appreciate the fact that Nurse Ratchet helped herself to some of my candy, more of the butterscotch than peppermint. It was clear she has a sweet tooth, but the bitch should have brought her own. I wanted to say something to her about it, but I took my bag and headed back to my room to hide them from everyone else.

I sat on the edge of my bed and thought over what just happened. Mom really came here asking for me to apologize for hurting my family when all of this started with her and her lack of ability to pick a better boyfriend. Tired and weak from not having anything to eat in days and the recent anger that surged through my body, I lay back onto the bed. I needed a nap. Hunger pangs made it harder for me to get comfortable but not harder for me to fall asleep.

I was awakened for dinner after what only seemed like an hour of sleep. I was hungry, but I didn't want to eat. As always, I just looked at the tray full of food they sat in front me in the cafeteria and sipped on the ice-cold beverage. I could hear the nurses whisper from across the room about my not eating. It was like they'd formed a plan on how they were going to get me to eat, so I just sat there until half of the lunchroom was clear and carried my tray over to the nurse who had to document how much I was eating before shoving the tray into a slot for discarding.

She gave me her usual reserved smile and told me I was good to go. I wanted to head back to my room but was told it was time for my therapy session with the good doctor.

Therapy? I said to myself. *For as long as I've been here, I have yet to have any type of therapy with anyone.*

One of the younger nurses knocked on the ajar door. A man resembling Santa Claus dressed in a blue button-down shirt and dark blue or maybe black khakis was seated, reading what I could only assume was my chart. He waved for me to come in and pointed to the chair. I looked down at it, cautiously sitting with my knees rubbing against one another and my hands clasped together, resting on them, as if I were about to pray.

He said nothing at first. He eyed me and my chart through his glasses that looked exactly like Benjamin Franklin's on the edge of his nose. He put my chart down, which was just a thin folder with a few pieces of paper in it and looked up at me while searching my face.

I looked down at the floor because I didn't like feeling awkward. Finally, he asked, "How are you doing here? Are you getting along with the other patients?"

I didn't know how to answer either of those questions because I was never meant to be there, so I shrugged my shoulders as a sign that I didn't want to answer his ridiculous question.

"I've heard that you haven't been eating, but if you don't eat or participate in therapy, you're going to be kept here a little while longer."

My right foot started to shake up and down, a habit of mine when I get nervous. While keeping my eyes glued to the floor, I could feel him studying me.

What he said next was a shocker. "If you have nothing else to say, then you can go now, but remember what I said."

I didn't even look up at him as I headed for the door. Careful not to look back, I didn't know if I should head to my room or to the activities room, which I had yet to be in since I'd been there. I decided to head to the activities room in hopes that if he saw me in there trying to make an effort, I wouldn't be forced to stay longer.

Over the next couple days, the words of the good doctor stayed with me. I realized I could be stuck in there. I wasn't even crazy. I just had a moment of weakness, and all the shit my mother had put me through over the years made me snap. It was all coming back to me, like constantly having to watch my siblings instead of being able to go outside and be a kid all because my mother wanted to party. I recalled my mother humiliating and bullying me when she had an audience, her choice in men, and the fact that I held her secret of her constant cheating when she brought other men back home.

There was such a buildup of lies, deception, bullying, and humiliation in and out of the home that I was surprised I didn't lose my cool a long time ago. But now… Now I had to prove myself worthy of being discharged before the good doctor decided otherwise, so I started being sociable to a few of the more sane patients and eating a few bites of my food here and there. I did what I had to do to get out. School would be starting back up pretty soon, and so far, my summer had been spent in the ICU and psych ward in my childhood home's hospital. It was the same hospital where my mother gave birth to me.

I made sure to do all the things I was supposed to in front of the nurses, so they saw that I was making an effort too. A few days later, I was released into the custody of my mother because I had nowhere else to go. I didn't even look like myself, let alone feel like myself. I had lost more than thirty pounds in the nine days that I was hospitalized because I couldn't keep anything down, nor would I eat, and I had constant diarrhea from the side effects of all the drugs they gave me.

Walking into my home was foreign to me. I didn't know how anyone would react to seeing me again or how I would react to seeing them. But everything was the same as the day I was kicked out. I don't know what I expected, but it was calmer than I'd thought it would be.

Eager to lie down on a real mattress, I walked straight up to my room. The hospital gave me the clothes I had arrived in. Luckily, they didn't have to cut them off of me. But I couldn't fit them anymore either. I'd always said I wanted to lose weight to become more appealing, but I never thought it would happen the way it did.

I showered before I was discharged that morning, but there is nothing quite like taking a shower in the comfort of your own home—or at least I thought it was my home. Mom didn't say a word on the way there, as I'd hoped, and all I did was stare out the window into oblivion.

I quickly undressed and threw my clothes to the side to be washed, even though the hospital had done that for me already. I wrapped the fitted towel around me, amazed that at one point this towel didn't even fit half of me, let alone all of me. Everything felt like an out-of-body experience.

I flipped the switched on the wall that brought the lightbulb above to life and headed downstairs to the bathroom. I felt a little bit lighter on my feet, but I tried not to let this moment get to me because it was only my first day home in weeks, and I still didn't know how the rest of the house would handle my being home and what I had done.

I made it down the stairs to my sister's room, where she was still sitting on her chair, looking in the mirror, and doing her hair. She glanced up at me as I passed through, but she didn't say a word. Raven, on the other hand, was excitedly eager to know where I was going so soon.

"I'm going to take a shower," I said.

"Take a shower?" she asked with a grin on her face.

"Yes."

She stuck her pointer finger in her mouth, giggled, and lay back down to watch her show.

Walking into the hallway, I caught the last part of Mom and Devon's conversation from downstairs. "She didn't say anything the whole way over here," I heard Mom say.

Why would she say this to Devon? Why in the hell would he care? He was part of the reason things went the way they did in the first place. I ignored the rest of the conversation and walked into the bathroom. I shut the door behind me and hung up my towel before turning on the water.

I just stood there naked, staring at myself in the mirror, not even recognizing myself. I had severe dark circles under my eyes like I hadn't slept in days, and my face was sunken in from hunger. I wasn't as fat as I used to be, but it still wasn't appealing to the naked eye. I didn't know what to think of myself at that point. All I knew for sure was that I really wanted to take a hot shower. My washcloth was still in the same place as the day I left, letting me know that either no one bothered to wash clothes, or they left what was mine in its place in hopes that I'd be back at some point.

I grabbed the washcloth and threw it to the side for a fresh one from the linen closet. Stepping into the back of the shower, I welcomed the heat and all of its glory. The heat of the shower never felt so damn good on my skin. There was a difference in the feel of the water in the hospital than at home.

I just stood there in the middle of the heavy stream of water. Taking it all in, I closed my eyes to reflect on all that had happened during the last week and a half. I didn't know how I felt about being home just yet, but I sure was happy to be out of the hospital.

I quickly washed my full body while having flashbacks of how quickly the water in the hospital got cold after a few minutes. I was in and out of the shower in less than ten minutes. I remembered to dry my feet before touching the bathroom floor with my towel that was hanging on the hook next to the opening. Once my feet were completely dry, I grabbed my dirty clothes from the toilet lid and headed for the door. I was out of the bathroom and back upstairs in my room in the blink of an eye, and I noticed that I wasn't so out of breath.

I dried off and dressed in record time, hung my towel back up on the vanity mirror, and looked around my room while wondering what to do next. I grabbed my remote and switched the TV on. I looked down at the remote and smiled to myself because I had to ask for permission to watch TV in the hospital. *Not anymore*, I said to myself. I turned to my usual channel, the Food Network, and sunk myself into the bed while pulling the covers up to my chin.

In that moment, it felt like I was home. I wasn't thinking about who was downstairs or what was being said or how things had been between my mother and me. But that moment right there felt like home to me.

I was so lost in what was on TV that it never occurred to me to check my phone. I had to charge it when I came home because it was completely dead when I got it back from the hospital. I don't know why I was so worried about it because it wasn't like I had anyone to talk to anyway. I hadn't seen or heard from my cousin since the day I was hauled away in the ambulance, and it wasn't like she'd want to speak to me now.

So, I turned my phone back on and set it back on my nightstand. The phone sprang to life, letting me know that it was charging. I rolled back over and faced the TV when my phone started vibrating uncontrollably. Confused by the multiple vibrations, I grabbed my phone and stared at the screen. There were no text messages, as if I were surprised.

No, I'd just forgotten that I had turned on every notification on my phone.

Once the buzzing and vibrating stopped, I laid my phone back down on my nightstand. "Hmm. No text from my cousin Jessica." I didn't know why I'd expect her to ever text me again after what I'd done to her family. I wouldn't text or call me either because what do you say to a person you found passed out on your kitchen floor with an empty pill bottle right next to them? *Hi, so glad you're alive?* Or maybe she didn't know I was out of the hospital yet.

Either way, I wouldn't even know what to say to her to begin with. But it didn't matter anyway. I was tired—tired like I hadn't slept in days or weeks.

Lying in my bed seemed to put my body at ease because before I knew it, I was asleep. I don't know how long I slept, but it wasn't long before my sister started yelling from the bottom of the stairs that dinner was done.

"Ok. I'll be down soon," I yelled back. But I was exhausted, so I closed my eyes once more. When I heard her shut my door from below, I knew I didn't have long before someone else would come knocking, so I gave myself ten more minutes before I went down.

The allotted time turned to fifteen, and then fifteen turned into twenty, and by then I knew it was time to get up before they started to wonder. So, I slipped on a pair of socks that I received from the hospital. You know, the ones that have suction cups on the bottom. I had at least two pairs of them. Most people would have thrown away any and all evidence of being in a mental ward, but I kept those socks for some reason, and I wasn't ashamed of it. I mean, they were just socks, after all.

Smelling the beautiful aroma of homemade food, I tiredly stumbled my way down the stairs and out of the confines of my room. I knew it had only been about a week and a half, but I had forgotten what my mom's food tasted like. The smell of the food made my stomach churn, almost in pain, from the hunger. The closer I got to the kitchen, the louder my stomach growled for her food. I could tell from the smell of it that she'd made tacos or something close to it.

I entered the kitchen, shocked to see that it actually was tacos. Mom knew that there was nothing I loved more on this Earth than homemade tacos. Everyone was already seated at the table when I came in, and all eyes shot up in my direction like they'd just seen a ghost. I ignored the awkward moment and grabbed a paper plate from the stove. Trying to ignore the stares, I tried to think of what I wanted first—a taco salad or tacos.

I hadn't really had anything real or solid to eat, so I knew this was going to be good. So, I opted for tacos. I was starving, but I didn't know just how much food my stomach could handle at one time just yet since I'd lost so much weight. So, I decided to make two tacos since the tortilla shells were not your regular-sized shells. But I was one for presentation when it came to food, especially tacos, even though they are the messiest thing to eat.

After I'd finished making my plate, I sat down at the table, still being monitored like a lost child. I reached for a napkin and scanned the table at the same time. When I did, everyone quickly looked down at their plates like they'd just been caught. The awkwardness was starting to make me feel somewhat uncomfortable, so I tried to focus on my plate of food. I was so hungry I felt I could almost throw up before I even took my first bite of food.

I downed the first taco so quickly that I was barely breathing between bites. It was so good I could feel the sour cream on each side of my face, giving Raven something to laugh about because her face was always covered in food. She thought it was funny that now mine was too. I wiped both sides of my face with the heavy-duty napkin and looked down at my second taco like it was a mistake. I became full as fast as the first taco went down. With a shock of horror on my face, I never thought I'd see the day that I got full off of just one taco.

That was disappointing. I'd lost so much weight that my stomach couldn't hold any more food, and as much as I hated to waste food, especially tacos, I didn't know what I was going to do with the last one. So, I sat there and allowed my food a chance to digest. I figured that maybe when I ate too fast, I didn't give myself time to properly chew my food.

I folded my hands in my lap as I did in the hospital during therapy sessions and looked down at the floor, careful not to look up at my siblings. As much as I wanted to look at them, I couldn't bring myself to do it out of both embarrassment and disappointment in myself. I didn't want things to feel any more awkward than they already were, so I focused a lot on the floor and studied the white tile pattern. And when that got old, I quickly stretched my neck upward, admiring the popcorn paint on the walls and the ceiling. I wondered, *What's in the paint to make it popcorn-like, and how did they get it to actually stay on the ceiling and not on the floor?*

The longer I sat there, the more I realized just how full I truly was and that my stomach was not going to allow me to steal another bite after the last few, so I took a few more bites of the second taco so it wouldn't look like I'd wasted the whole thing, and then I tossed the rest in the trash. Ashamed, I made sure the plate landed upside down for no one to see. I'd never wasted food before, and my weight displayed it, but this time I had no choice.

Feeling foolish, I grabbed a water bottle from the fridge and headed upstairs.

On my way up the stairs, Mom's voice called out, "Was dinner was good?"

"Yes," I said. "It was very good, and I'm too full to eat more. Thank you!" Then I retreated back upstairs to my room where I spent the rest of the night consumed by guilt and shame—guilt for having done what I did to my siblings and shame for not being able to look at them. I was so depressed over it that all I wanted to do was just sleep the rest of the night away, but I was full from eating one-and-a-half tacos that I couldn't get comfortable for a moment to lie down.

So, I sat halfway up in the bed with my back pressed against the headboard and the rest of my body slumped over like a drunk on a Friday night at an all-you-can-drink pub. After maybe half an hour of TV time, I decided to leave the TV on and let it watch me watch the backs of my eyelids when the food eventually settled, and I was able to lie down the rest of the night. Even after the little nap I had before dinner, I was still able to go back to sleep for the rest of the night and sleep soundly.

The summer days flew by just as quickly as they came, even though I'd spent the majority of them in a psych ward. But fall was approaching, and it was soon time for me to go back to school. And just as quickly as everything else flew by, so did the ice between me and my family. No one had a reason to tiptoe around me anymore, Mom was back to her bullying, humiliating ways, and I was school shopping for supplies and an iPad or mini laptop computer to help with work during the schoolyear.

I rushed home, in excitement, to tell my mom that the school was actually giving out iPads or mini laptops to help with homework, and she was just as shocked as I was to learn of this. But when I told her that we also had the option of getting both, she told me I should go back and get the other one. I explained that it came out of our financial aid and that I didn't want to be greedy. It was the first day the school had opened its school supply store.

She yelled at me like I had done something wrong. "You're being selfish for not going back to get the mini laptop!" she said. "I could have sold it for money."

Devon quickly agreed when he heard her idea. "We could've gotten a lot of money for it."

"Get out of my face," my mom commanded me.

I was so excited to get home and show my mother what I had bought in preparation for the new school year, but my joy was quickly short-lived when I was called "selfish" for not wanting to spend all of my aid so she could make a quick buck.

I quickly turned to retreat upstairs to my room. I fought the urge to cry, but the tightening of my face and the trembling of my lips were making it impossible to hold back the tears. I held back for as long as I could until I was in the confines of my own room. I'd been called "selfish" for something that was going to benefit her.

I sat on the edge of my bed and cried. I didn't understand it. After all that my mother had put me through, I still felt the need to please her. I was excited and thought it was mighty big of my new school to be doing something like that for the students. But there I was, crying in my room, because no matter how many times she put me down, I still felt the need to share my joy with my mother only for her to shut me down. I didn't understand why I kept going back to this same old song and dance, but at the same time, she was my mother, and no matter how many times she knocked me down, I still got back up.

I realized that my mother and I may never have a normal mother-daughter relationship, and no matter how hard I try to please and make her happy, it may be time to face the fact that it may never happen. Trying to crack a smile through my tears, I dried my face and unloaded my backpack. But trying to smile through the pain only made my face look like it was having a stroke.

Blinded by the tears once more, I started color coding my folders according to my class schedule. Once I'd finished, I neatly packed my bag away and sat it gently in the corner, too exhausted from crying to even check out my new iPad. After being called "selfish," I decided it was only best if I stayed up in my room for the rest of the night to avoid tension. I turned on the TV and curled up in a ball under the covers.

We would end up spending three more summers in that place. Three more birthdays, three more holidays, and three more reasons for me to hate myself over and over again. We moved into another house up the street from where we lived, only this time, I didn't end up in the attic. I know it's weird to think, but I felt some kind of special for living in a house—and not just any house but a brownstone, which was something I'd always said I wanted to live in when I got out on my own. But also, for once, we weren't living in a cramped apartment or a trailer full of rodents.

A month and a half after moving into our new house, Devon and I got into another argument, and once again, my mom took his side. Only this time, there was no coming back for me. Mom made that clear when she called it "tough love." I was just one month shy of my twenty-second birthday.

Jessica had already gotten a little place of her own with her boyfriend. They didn't have much, but they made the best of it. It was a cute little duplex. So once again, I packed all I had into as many bags as I could carry and moved in with my cousin and her boyfriend.

When I wasn't working three jobs and going to school full time, I slept there on a small mattress that she made up for me on the living room floor. Her Labrador had favored that mattress more than I. He liked to wait until I would get up to go to the bathroom or to shower for work to sneak onto the mattress and lie down. Even though he had a whole bed to himself, that dog loved that damn mattress, but it was where I laid my head for the better part of three months.

It was the first time I had ever missed my birthday and the holidays with my family, but I made the best of it while I was there. It gave me a chance to save up for a place of my own. But all everyone else could see was that I was still living with my cousin three months later and not paying a damn bill. They didn't know that I kept the water on when my cousin and her boyfriend couldn't.

I guess they forgot to mention that part to everybody who felt the need to criticize me, but I'd learned over the years that you couldn't do good for everybody, especially when you were the one in need. But by the grace of God and prayer every night, by the end of December, I received word that I was approved for a small two-bedroom townhome. It couldn't have come at a better time for me. I was getting tired of being awakened by the sound of my cousin and her boyfriend having sex almost every night. They were ready to have their place back, and I was ready to give it to them. I was due to move into my townhome by the first week in January.

I was scared and a nervous wreck but excited at the same time and ready for this to happen. I guess it was good that I never got too comfortable living with my cousin because it never gave me the chance to unpack my plastic bags. Everything I had was in four large, black trash bags, and I finally had something good going for me.

After being kicked out of my home twice by my mother for the love of her man, the attempted suicide, and the years of bullying and humiliation, I happily moved into my new home on the sixth of January with plenty of space to grow. I felt like I finally had it all.

But nothing lasts forever, does it? Otherwise, I wouldn't have found myself losing what I thought was going to be my "forever home" less than two years later after giving myself to a boy (not a man) whom I thought loved me. I wouldn't have spent the next year traveling from couch to floor trying to find solidarity and meaning in my life. I was young and dumb to have taken him back more times than he deserved with the promise of a better life and a ring that could take the breath of an asthmatic away. But it ended up slapping me in the face in the end because no one chooses to wind up in a Motel 6, forced to make it the temporary home it was never meant to be.

About the Author

Tozaneé Smith is a teacher, a mother, a nurse, and a cook (at heart). She loves spending time at home on the couch with a good romance novel and an occasional glass of wine. Every now and again, Tozaneé likes to spend quality time with close personal friends in her hometown of Martinsburg, WV and enjoys going to the movies and on long road trips.

Acknowledgments

I would like to acknowledge Sherian Brown and Shaundale Rénā for all of their hard work and dedication in making my story come to life. Without them I'd still be hiding behind my words. (Oh, that's sexy. I like that!)

I'd also like to acknowledge Sandy, Sue, Pamela, Chelsea, Crystal and Heidi for always putting up with my craziness and for always being around when I needed you most. You ladies mean everything to me, and I thank all of you from the bottom of my heart.

Made in the USA
Middletown, DE
25 March 2024